二十四連環腿法

24 RUNNING FOOT STROKES

李英昂編著

By **Lee Ying Arng**

香港 藝美圖書公司 出版

Yih Mei Book Co.

24 RUNNING FOOT STROKES

Writer: *Lee Ying Arng*

Publisher & Distributor: Yih Mei Book Co.
No. 7, Tin Lok Lane Ground Fl.
Wanchai, Hong Kong.
Tel.: 3-750240

© Yih Mei Book Co.

First Edition December, 1984.

Second Edition April, 1987.

二 十 四 連 環 腿 法

附： 練 腿 基 本 功

編著者： 李　英　昂

出版兼
發行者： 藝 美 圖 書 公 司

香港灣仔天樂里七號地下
電話：5-750240

承印者： 嶺 南 印 刷 公 司

香港西環第二街 129 號

一九八七年四月第二版

版 權 所 有 · 翻 印 必 究

（圖書目錄函索即寄）

自　序

　　腿擊法，乃我國武術中一種盡量發揮强有力下肢功用之術。以世界各國之武術言，除日本之「柔道」，法國之「踢腿術」（LA SAVATE），及美國之「摔角術」（WRESTLING）等略具腿擊之法外，我國武術中完備之腿擊法，可言睥睨一切同道矣。

　　腿擊法，在我國北派武術，尤爲重視，被認爲創人取勝之無上法門。所以有「手是兩扇門，全憑脚打人」，「手打三分，脚打七分」之諺。惜乎腿法雖妙，但雜於各家，毫無系統使人學習；且各派名家之妙着，又不肯公開，致大好國術精華，逐漸解體失傳，擅者日鮮，實使愛好國術者，爲之扼腕。

　　不佞年前有見及此，以個人有限之精力，虛心訪求，集各家武術之腿法精華，類而編之，總成「腿法十三訣」，更編「二十四腿擊要法」。本書編排，由淺入深，每一腿法，皆採猛烈實用，輕則使敵受創，重則使敵喪生；並製圖詳釋，務求簡明，使好此道者，易於接受。本書

I

AUTHOR'S PREFACE

Foot striking is one of Chinese martial arts that gives full play to the powerful functions of the lower limbs. So far as the martial arts of all nations in the world are concerned, except the Japanese Judo, la savate of France and U.S. wrestling which contain some foot strokes, the perfect foot striking techniques in Chinese martial arts can be said to be overwhelming.

In particular, the northern schools of Chinese martial arts take foot striking seriously and regard it as a supreme trick for beating opponents, thus giving rise to the proverbs: "Hands are two doors while feet are used for striking" and "Hand striking makes up 30% while foot striking accounts for 70%". It is a pity that although foot striking techniques are wonderful, they are confused and varied among schools and too unsystematic to learn. And famous masters of each school are mostly unwilling to make public their clever tricks. Therefore, the excellent cream of Chinese martial arts has gradually become disintegrated and even lost. As they have not been widely spread, the skilled have got fewer and fewer, which has indeed made those who love Chinese martial arts feel sorry about this situation.

In view of the above-mentioned facts, although I am not skilled, I have, since about one year ago, searched modestly for the essences of the foot striking techniques of various schools of Chinese martial arts, availing myself of my limited vigour and ability. I compiled and classified them into the book "Thirteen Foot Striking Tricks" and further into the book "Twenty-four Main Foot Striking Techniques". I have arranged the foot striking techniques from the easy to the difficult. Every technique I have selected is both violent and practical,

不敢說發前人所未述，但至少能令好此者得一門徑；高明之士，幸勿以其淺陋見笑。本書得胡廣池兄演式，黃超強兄攝影，十分感激，特此致謝。是為序。

李英昂　序於爐峯

中華塊寶

which can injure an opponent if light force is exerted and kill him if heavy force is used. Illustrations are provided herewith to explain the techniques in detail. I have tried my best to make my explanations brief and clear so as to be easily accepted by those who are fond of the art. I dare not say that I have said what have not been said by my predecessors, but at least my explanations can provide the fans with a key. I hope that the better qualified will not laugh at their meagreness. We are grateful that Mr. Wu Kwong Chih has made the demonstration and Mr. Wong Chiu Keung has taken the photos. The foregoing is my preface of this book.

By Lee Ying Arng at the Peak of Hong Kong.

目　錄　CONTENTS

腿法談要

技擊以五法爲基，故必先明五法，而後武功始有成就。五法者，手法、眼法、身法、腿法及步法也。

五法以步爲主，手、眼、身、腿次之。蓋無步法，任何神拳妙技，亦必寸步難移；既寸步難移，則手法雖極神奇，亦將歸無效，不能施之於敵。且步法不靈，腿法亦隨之無用；腿法不能變化，則身法滯笨；身法滯，則眼法無從練，手法亦無從施矣。故云步法爲五法之主。然五法亦應合一，方能運用靈巧。至主要運用，則以腿法之實力最猛，且腿法出擊，不但可出奇制勝，腿之勁力亦超手勁數倍。故腿法爲南北武術家所重，北派武術尤甚。

談腿法，每有誤雜以步法者，其實腿法與步法大異，切勿視而爲一。腿法者，以膝、足尖、足跟、足側、腿內外側等部巧法擊人之術。而步法者，乃以下肢形成前進、後退、左閃、右躍，而使身法隨之能起落變轉者也。

或曰手較腿靈活，何捨手法而就腿法？是未明武技之理耳。武技應敵，一如兵法，以出奇制勝爲主；且萬事練之則靈，靈則巧，固不在乎手或腿也。平心而論，腿較手長，勁較手偉，且手法易爲敵忌，不若腿法之易爲敵疏。故腿法易於倏起忽沒，偷隙創敵，而收「出奇制勝，攻敵無備」之效。然仍須與手相應並用，不可偏廢，蓋腿法雖巧，亦須上影下蹴，聲東擊西，始能預收實效也。

1

THE MAIN POINTS OF FOOT STRIKING TECHNIQUES

The art of attack and defence is based on five categories of techniques. Only after understanding them can one make achievements in the martial arts. The five categories are: hand-moving techniques, looks of eyes, body-moving techniques, foot-striking techniques and footwork.

Among them, footwork is primary and the other four are secondary because if one has not mastered good footwork, it will be difficult for him or her to move a step even though he or she possesses wonderful tricks or techniques. In such circumstances, miraculous as hand-moving techniques are, they will become null and void and cannot be used to fight an opponent. If footwork does not work, foot-striking techniques will also be of no use. If foot-striking techniques are not variable, the movements of the body will seem to be stagnant and awkward. And if the body is stagnantly moved, looks of eyes cannot be practised and in turn the hand-moving techniques cannot be put to good use. Therefore, we say that footwork is the primary one of all the five categories. The five, however, must be integrated for the sake of nimble application. As for the importance in the application, the actual power of the foot-striking techniques is the most violent and striking with feet can defeat the enemy by a surprise move. Moreover, the force of feet is a few times greater than that of hands. Due to the foregoing, foot-striking is valued by the northern and southern masters of Chinese martial arts, especially by the northern schools.

With regard to foot-striking, it is often confused with foot-work. In fact, the former is greatly different from the latter and they should not be regarded as one. Foot-striking is an art for striking skilfully at someone with one knee, the toes,

腿法施敵，貴乎靈敏迅捷。蓋腿擊攻擊轉踢，旋起翻落之間，略有遲滯拙笨，實關係全身，不獨腿法無克敵之功，且極易為敵乘隙反制。是故用腿之先，應先加練腿；練腿之先，則又須練步。練至步法穩，則求兩腿柔化；待兩腿已達柔化之階，再求準度。能練至步子穩，方向適，重心吻，兩腿柔，則是時起腿飛擊，未有不靈敏迅捷者矣。

或曰兩腿柔何能創敵？是未明擊腿之道耳。古賢練腿，先吊、後擗、再踢，務求其柔而勁貫，靈而不拙。所謂：「擊人時，不着則柔，着人則創」者，非在拙力，而在彈勁；彈勁之求，則在兩腿柔而氣貫也。世有傳腿法者，使其徒日夜蠻踢木石，至木朽石毀，言腿法已成，欺人之談也。雖然腿力足斷木石，然失之拙笨，苟遇步法巧者，奈其腿擊不達何？當知腿擊之道，尚柔不尚剛，尚巧不尚拙也。

腿擊之法，各家各派，皆含一二，北派尤多。且有以腿法步法立派者，如外家之彈腿門，內家之八卦門等是。然以余考證所得，各家所含腿法，類其精要，不外余所定之點、蹬、割、擦、絆、挑、鈎、掃、絞、踩、剷、挾、撞等十三要訣，及二十四腿法範圍之內。

余所編之二十四腿法，以人體前後上中下三盤要害為的，而施以腿擊之法。其法可分二途：其一為輔助腿法，即於應敵之際，手法或有不及之時，而輔以腿法，俾竟全功。此種腿法，多不甚猛烈，只能創敵一時，蓋其主力，乃在手法也。其一為主用腿法，即於應敵之際，完全靠腿擊制敵，有時或用手法助之。此等腿法，猛烈非常，不動則已，動則傷人，甚且喪命也。至何時何地，應施何法，始克實效，此則在施者之隨時審察，

heel or one side of one foot, internal or lateral side of one leg, etc.; while footwork means that the lower limbs make such movements as moving forward, drawing back, dodging to the left and leaping to the right, which in turn enable the body to turn, following the dropping of the foot.

Somebody may say that hands are quicker than feet and then ask why feet are used instead of hands. This is because he or she doesn't know the principles of martial arts. Just as the art of war, in meeting an opponent, the stress of martial arts is laid on defeating him by a surprise move. You will become clever at everything so long as you practise regularly in it and you will further become skilful, never mind whether you use hads or feet. In all fairness, legs are longer than arms and the power of one foot is greater than that of one hand; an opponent will easily get prepared for the attack with hands but be liable to neglect any foot stroke. Therefore, it is easy to snap a foot out swiftly and draw it back quickly. Thus you can snatch a good chance and beat the opponent so as to attain the effect of "striking when or where an opponent is unprepared and defeating him by a surprise move". Nevertheless, feet must be used correspondingly and simultaneously with hands and neither of them can be overemphasized at the expense of the other because although you may have clever foot striking techniques, you can obtain real effects only by pretending to strike with hands but actually kicking and by making a feint to the east but attacking in the west.

In fighting an opponent by means of foot striking, the important thing is agility because a little stagnancy or awkwardness during the movements of feet such as striking, turning, kicking, leaping or dropping has an actual bearing on the whole body, not only causing foot striking to lose its effect of defeating the opponent, but easily giving him a chance to counter-defeat you. Therefore, prior to using your feet, exercise yourself in leg training, before which, exercise yourself first in footwork. Having got your footwork steady try to make both legs flexible, after which, try to be accurate. When the steps are steady, the directions are right, the centre of gravity is coincident and the

4

相機而行，固不能執一而論也。

功夫不負有心人

legs are flexible, you will become quick and nimble in kicking.

Somebody may ask how the flexible legs can be used to beat an opponent. This is because he or she does not know the principles of foot-striking. Ancient able persons exercised themselves in leg training by suspending, splitting and snapping for the purpose to make them flexible (i.e. to make them agile and not awkward) and concentrate strength. The saying that "when attacking an opponent, the strokes turn gentle when they miss the mark but injure him when they hit the mark" does not lay stress on clumsy forces but gives emphasis to elastic forces. An elastic force is based on the flexibility of legs and the concentration of strength. Some persons on earth who teach foot striking techniques make their disciples kick recklessly against wood or stone day and night, and when wood or stone is broken, the disciples are told that they have succeeded in mastering the techniques, which is actually a deceptive talk. Although the strength of feet is adequate for breaking wood or stone, it still has the defect of being too awkward. If they meet persons whose footwork is nimble and skilful, what can they do as their feet cannot hit the opponents in any way? It should be understood that the stress of foot striking is laid on flexibility and not on rigidity as well as on nimbleness and not on awkwardness.

Every school of Chinese martial arts has a few foot striking techniques and a northern school has even more. Some schools are even established on the basis of footwork and foot striking techniques, such as the Foot Snapping Sect of the School that emphasizes the exercises to benefit bones and muscles, the Eight Diagrams Sect of the School that emphasizes the exercises to benefit the intended transfer of strength inside the body, etc.. However, according to my personal research, among the foot striking techniques of every school, the essential ones are nothing·more than the thirteen important tricks defined by me, i.e. shoving, straight-kicking, cutting, shaving, snapping, tripping, picking, hooking, sweeping, clipping, stamping, bumping and clamping, and they are also within the twenty-four foot striking techniques.

6

The twenty-four foot striking techniques compiled by me are used to kick at the vital parts in the upper, middle and lower sections of the front and back of a human body. These techniques can be grouped into two: auxiliary ones used to assist hands in striking the opponent when it is unable to beat the opponent merely with hands, and with this assistance, you can defeat him completely, in most cases, the techniques are not violent enough and can only make the opponent lose the fight temporarily because the emphasis is laid on striking him with hands; main ones which mean that feet are wholly relied upon in the fight, sometimes assisted by hands, and these techniques are so violent as to injure or even kill the opponent. As regards what technique a user should use to obtain actual results and when or where he should use it, they depend upon the user's ability to judge the situation at any moment and act accordingly. This should not be treated as all the same.

腿勁釋義

　　腿勁起於腰際，使氣貫於膝、小腿、足尖、足跟等部，而運用十三要訣施之。腿法勁路有上、下、直、橫、斜等五種，而以「彈勁」納之。茲將五種勁路，釋義如下：

上勁　　上勁者，上踢之勁也。上踢時，先略曲一腿，坐腰弓背，蓄勁於腰際丹田。起腿之際，集中意志，氣貫於足，而後上踢，其勁始整。

　　踢腿擊敵，非但要勁貫神集，尤要有彈勁。所謂彈勁者，有伸縮回力之勁也。今例釋之：設我欲起腿踢敵之手部，起腿施勁，非若一般拳家之一始即鼓全勁，乃漸漸施勁，至達目的，而後始發全勁，免未達目的前傷氣耗勁之舉，是為發勁之上法。

　　腿勁一發，既達目的，即借踢敵時之反挫力回彈；彈縮之勁，與踢出之勁適反，其回彈之時，即施全彈。所謂：「五百觔力出，亦須五百觔力回」者，即彈勁之寫眞也。

　　見第一圖，線條之粗者，乃代表偉勁；線條之細者，乃代表弱勁。A代表發腿，B代表收腿。

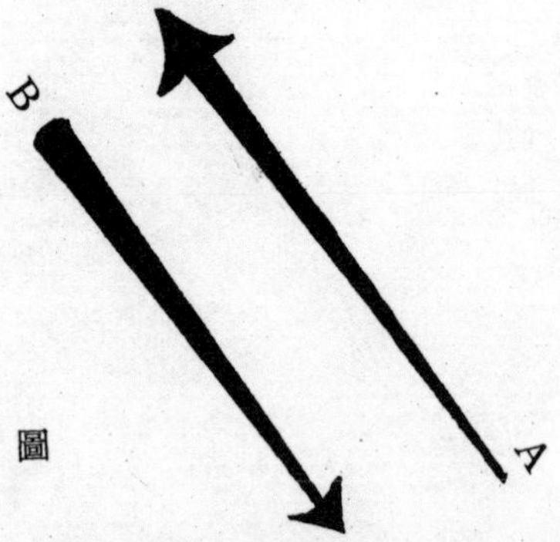

第　一　圖
Fig. 1

THE DEFINITIONS OF FOOT FORCES

Originating between the loins, foot forces transfer and concentrate onto such parts as knee, shank, toes, heel, etc.. These forces are to be exerted in accordance with the thirteen important tricks compiled by me. There are five modes of kicking: upward, downward, straight, transverse and slanting, which are generally called "snapping forces". Now let me define these five modes as follows:–

Upward Force: An upward force is that in kicking up. When doing so, bend a leg slightly, lower the waist and hump the back, retaining your strength between the loins. When you are about to snap one foot up, concentrate your mind and strength onto it; then snap it up, exerting the right force. When kicking at an opponent, you not only should centre your mind and strenth, but should, in particular, use an elastic force, which means the force that can be freely stretched out and drawn back. For example, if I am going to kick at an opponent's hand, I do not exert all my force at once from the beginning as general boxers but exert it gradually until the target is hit and then give full play to it, lest the force should be wasted before reaching the target. This is the best method of the exertion of forces.

When the outgoing force reaches the target, it rebounds by means of the recoil force resulting from kicking up. The recoil force goes in the direction just opposite to that of the outgoing one. When the force rebounds, give full play to it. The saying that "if 500 catties of force is exerted, 500 catties of force should return" is the real description of an elastic force.

See Fig. 1. The thick parts of the lines represent strong forces, while the thin ones represent weaker forces. "A" is the starting point from which the foot is snapped out and "B" is the starting point from which the foot is drawn back.

9

下勁 下勁者，下跺之勁也。下跺時，設欲跺左足，則腿隨身向上略挺，左膝略曲，提起左足，勁蓄於腰際丹田，氣貫左足跟，集中意志，不施則已，施用則突隨身向下坐之勢，左足下跺。

跺時，意志要集而有勁彈。集中精神，而後勁能氣貫；有彈勁，跺後始能即變步化式，以免滯呆。

直勁 直勁者，直踢之勁也。直踢時，勁須貫前，其法一腿略弓，坐腰弓背，勁蓄於腰際丹田；一腿彎曲，提膝向上，集中意志，勁貫於足，施小腿勁，向前踢出。踢達目的，即使彈勁縮回，以待換勁。

橫勁 橫勁者，橫踹之勁也。橫勁較上、下、直等勁為難施。此法非腿真柔，切戒輕用。橫踹時，其先略曲一腿，坐腰弓背，蓄勁於腰際丹田，而後集中意志，勁貫於足，配合上身略傾之勢（起右腿，則身左傾；起左腿，則身右傾；因一傾之勢，起腿踹敵，易使勁貫於足也），突起腿橫踹，踹達目的，切勿停勁，應立即使彈勁縮回，以待換勁，且免被敵所乘。

斜勁 斜勁者，斜彈之勁也。斜彈之勁，較橫勁尤難施。橫勁施用，尚可借着身勢，而斜彈勁，乃純靠小腿之勁者。

斜彈勁使用，並無定法。或斜中正取，或斜中橫取，或斜中上取，或斜中下取，或斜中中取，或斜中圈取。

斜彈勁之施於腿法，多在使手或腿法取敵之際，被敵換式閃過，而即乘其換式之際，舊力已過，新力

Downward Force: A downward force is the force in kicking down. If the left foot is to kick down, lift the left leg slightly up together with the body, bend the knee and lift and left foot; storing your strength between the loins, transfering and concentrating it onto the left heel and centering your mind, snap the left foot downward suddenly, following the lowering of the body.

When kicking down, Centre your mind and exert an elastic force. Only by centering your mind can your strength be concentrated. Only by exerting an elastic force can the foot-work and posture be variable to avoid stagnancy or awkward-ness.

Straight Force: A straight force is the force in kicking straight forward. When kicking straight forward, concentrate your strength to the front. Bowing one leg slightly, lowering the waist, humping the back and storing your strength between the loins, bend the other leg, lift the knee up, centre your mind, concentrate your strength onto the foot, exert the force of the shank and snap the foot out forward. As soon as the foot reaches the target, draw it back by means of an elastic force so as to transfer the strength.

Transverse Force: A transverse force is the force in kicking transversely. The transverse force is more difficult to exert than the upward, downward and straight forces. Don't use it rashly if you have not got your legs really flexible. When kicking transversely, bend one leg slightly, lower the waist, hump the back, store your strength between the loins, then centre your mind, transfer your strength to the foot and snap it transversely suddenly, following the slight inclination of the upper body. (When the right leg is lifted, the body inclines to the right, and vice versa. Due to the inclination, it is easy to transfer the strength onto the foot in kicking against the opponent.) When the foot hits the target, don't cease the exertion of force but draw the foot back at once by means of an elastic force so as to transfer the strength and prevent the opponent from taking advantage of the opportunity.

未生，難爲招架之時，突變腿法，以斜彈勁取之，
攻其不能備。故施用之際，全在乘機取巧，而尤須
換勁迅速，是所以較橫勁尤難者也。

夏練三伏　　　冬練三九

Slanting Force: A slanting force is the force in kicking slantingly. It is even more difficult to exert a slanting force than a transverse force. When exerting a transverse force, you can still take advantage of the inclination of the body. But the exertion of a slanting force relies merely on the force of the shank. There are not any definite methods for using the slanting force. You may snap the foot out slantingly, aiming straight forward, transversely, upward, downward, centrally or circularly at your target.

In foot striking techniques, the exertion of a slanting force mostly occur at the time when the opponent changes his posture and dodges your attack with one hand or foot. At that time, the opponent has just used up his old force and not brought forth his new force yet, which is the point when he is difficult to ward off any blows. If you change your foot-striking techniques and kick at the opponent by means of a slanting force at this moment, you can defeat him when he had not got ready yet. Therefore, when exerting such a force, you must seize any chance to gain advantage and change your strength swiftly. This is why it is even more difficult to exert a slanting force than a transverse one.

練腿法要

　　練腿之道，各家各派不同，然總其大要，不外吊、擗、踢三要訣及死、活二大派。

　　死法練腿，如前所述之踢樁等法是，純以死功剛勁為主，最不可取，習之非但無益，且常致害。

　　至於活法練腿，其練法純主自然，先練腿軟，次練勁貫，再練彈勁。如此循序漸進，使兩腿柔剛並濟，運用靈活，為練腿功之正道。

　　練腿季候，宜在冬夏二季，以夏季練之尤易成功。古賢云：「夏練三伏，冬練三九」者，即指此。其必須擇夏季行功者，取其時筋骨因氣候關係，易於鬆軟之故。至冬練三九者，蓋冬季天氣寒冷，三九尤甚。人體各部筋骨，因氣候影響而起收縮作用，是時倘不勤加行功，則三伏所得，恐在三九失去。故古賢練拳行功，皆特重夏之三伏，冬之三九也。練腿行功之先後，應略行預備動作，以鬆活各部筋骨，免致有其他不良生理弊病。普通練腿，行功之先，應先略「曲膝蹲」三五次。如第二圖。

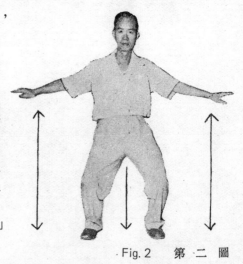

Fig. 2　第　二　圖

14

THE MAIN METHODS OF
LEG TRAINING

Each sect or school has different ways of training in legs, but the major ones can be summed up as nothing more than three important tricks, i.e. suspending, splitting and snapping, and two major schools, i.e. the dead and lively schools.

The dead method of leg training, such as kicking at a wood pile, purely gives emphasis to dead skills and rigid forces. It is the least desirable method. The training in it is not only of no use, but often harmful.

The lively method of leg training, however, is just contrary and purely gives emphasis to nature. In this training, one has to practise step by step from making legs flexible, transfering strength to feet to brining forth an elastic force so as to make two legs both rigid and flexible and enable them to be nimbly used. This is the right way of leg training.

The proper seasons for leg training are summer and winter. Especially in summer, it is easier to succeed in leg training. This is what the ancient able man's saying that "train in the hottest days of summer and in the coldest days of winter" meant. The reason to choose summer for training is that bones and tendons are liable to become flexible at that time due to the climate. The choice of the colest days of winter, however, is because in those days the bones and tendons of a human body contract due to the influence of the climate. If one does not train hard at that time, the results obtained in the hottest days will lose. Therefore, our ancient able predecessors took the hottest days of summer and the coldest days of winter seriously in their training in Chinese martial arts.

Before and after leg training, you have to carry out some preparatory exercises so as to loosen and activize the bones and tendons of every part and to avoid other harmful physio-

行功之後，應往來溜腿（溜腿者，乃 北方土語，即南方所謂散步，或鬆腿之謂）數趟。古賢所云：「打拳不溜腿，終是冒失鬼。」語雖俚俗，實有至理也，切勿以等閒視之。

　　茲將練功要法，分述如下：

吊 腿 法

　　吊腿行功，以能練至口可含足尖爲準。

　　吊腿之法，分正吊及側吊兩途。應先行側吊之法，待有相當成就，而後行正吊之法。

　　側吊之法至易。先備一木架（以書桅代之即可），高與己之臍齊，略作行功前準備運動後，將己足部，向上伸搭於架上，側身以上身向側下漸漸躬彎，而向側前伸探。如是練習，能練至身向側探，使肩與膝相觸爲止。早晚行功各一次，每次行功至乏不可耐時，則左右互易，行功畢，往來溜腿十數趟，以活筋骨血脈。依法練習，普通年齡未滿三十者，冬季九日，夏季七日，必然成功。功成後，進而即可行正面吊腿之法。見第三圖。

第 三 圖

Fig. 3

16

logical disadvantages. Generally, prior to leg training, you have to bend your knees and squat down 3 to 5 times as in Fig. 2. After training, you have to take a stroll to and fro several times. The saying of an ancient able man that "one is after all a harum-scarum if he or she does not take a stroll after boxing" is actually a golden dictum although it is rather vulgar and should not be treated lightly.

Now let me explain the important methods of training as follows:—

LEG SUSPENDING

The training in leg suspending aims at the ability to keep the tip of the foot in the mouth.

There are tow ways of leg suspending: front suspending and side suspending. Side suspending must be done first and front suspending is to be carried out after you have made considerable achievements in former.

Side suspending is very easy. Getting a wooden shelf (or desk) ready which is as tall as your navel, do some preparatory exercises before training, stretch your foot up and put it on the sheld and incline your upper body gradually down to the side, stretching it forward sidewise. Train continuously in this way until the body can be stretched to the side to make the shoulder touch the knee. Do this exercise once in the morning and once at night. If you feel too tired to go on, change the other side to train. After training, take a stroll to and fro a dozen times to make free the bones, tendons and blood vessels. Training according to this method, those under thirty of ages will surely succeed if they train for nine days in winter and seven days in summer. After you succeed in side suspending, you may further train in front suspending. See Fig. 3.

Front suspending and side suspending are only different in their directions. After doing some preparatory movements, stretch and put one foot on the wooden shelf, and holding the sole with both hands, bow the upper body to the front, increasing the force gradually. If you feel too tired to train

17

正面吊腿之法，與側身吊腿法，只方向不同耳。其法於略做預備運動後，將己欲練之腿，伸搭於木架之上，雙手捧住足心，正身向前向下躬探，漸漸行功，若感乏不可耐時，則左右腿互易練習，至兩腿力將盡，則停止練習，切勿過累。行功畢，往來溜腿十數趟，以鬆活各部筋骨及血脈。如是練習，至足尖能與頭頂相合，口可含足尖爲止。見第四圖。依法每日早晚行功各一次，普通年齡未滿三十者，冬季三月，夏季月半，即可成功。此階段練成功，則腿之根基已定，再進而練習擘腿，易如反掌矣。

第 四 圖　Fig. 4

擘 腿 法

擘腿行功，乃開胯拔筋，及練兩腿堅强而有彈性之法。以能練至兩腿能擘一字貼地，不須假借他力，使兩腿一彈而起爲準。

擘腿之法甚易。行功之先，略行膝蹲預備運動數次，以鬆

with the foot, change the other leg to go on until both legs are about to be exhausted, stop the exercise and don't make them too tired. After training, take a stroll to and fro a dozen times so as to make free the bones, tendons and blood vessels of every part. Train in this way until the forehead can touch the tip of the foot and can keep it in the mouth. See Fig. 4. Training daily in accordance with this method once in the morning and once at night, those under thirty of ages will be able to succeed if they train for three months in winter and one month and a half in summer. If you succeed in this step, you will have laid the foundation for leg training and it is as easy as turning your hand over to further train in leg splitting.

LEG SPLITTING

Training in leg splitting is a method to open the hip and pull the sinews as well as make both legs firm and elastic. It aims at the result that both legs can do a level split on the ground and then bounce up to stand without any external assistance.

Leg splitting is very easy. Before the exercise, do some preparatory movements of squatting a few times to make free blood vessels. Then standing akimbo, separate both legs as wide as about one metre (in case of an adult), lower the body and bend the left leg as if riding on a horse; stretch the right leg to the right, keeping the sole on the ground; incline the body to the right and press the right leg down as much as you can scores of times until you are about to be exhausted. See Fig. 5.

After splitting the right leg, go on with training in the left leg as follows: Draw the right leg back and bend it as if riding on a horse; then stretch the left leg to the left, keeping the foot on the ground; incline the body to the left and press the left leg down as much as you can scores of times until you are about to be exhausted. See Fig. 6.

After splitting the left leg, return to the right one in the way as aforesaid. Train alternately in this way until you feel exhausted. Then squat down as if Fig. 2 a few times, rise to your feet and take a stroll to and fro scores of times so as to

活血脈。而後兩手握拳置腰兩側，兩腿分開，約三四尺寬（成人計）將身下坐，先屈左腿，如坐馬式；再向右直伸右腿，足心不可離地，身向右側。盡量向下擗右腿數十下，至力將盡為止。見第五圖。

承上擗完右腿，可繼而練左腿。其法收右腿，屈如坐馬式，然後向左伸左腿，足心不可離地，身向左側。盡量向下擗左腿數十下，至力將盡為止。見第六圖。

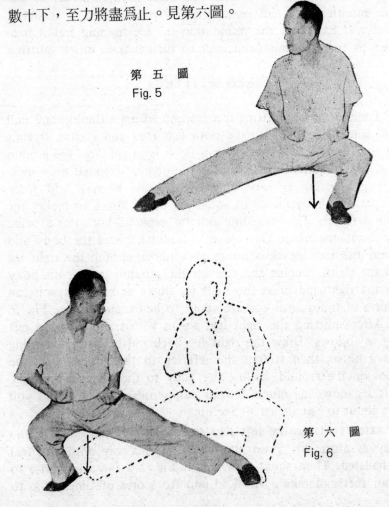

第 五 圖
Fig. 5

第 六 圖
Fig. 6

loosen the sinews and promote blood circulation as well as avoid imbalance.

This exercise can be done once in the morning and once at night and can be done together with leg suspending. In general, those under thirty of ages will be able to succeed if they train for one month in summer and one and a half months in winter. After you succeed in this exercise, the tendons and muscles of your legs will not only become firm and flexible, but be rich in elasticity. When you snap one foot up, it will come as high as the forehead (be aware that if your foot comes above the head, it is not really flexible) and when you stretch one leg down, it will be close to the ground. Those who exericse in leg training should avoid victory fondness by all means. Being over-anxious for quick success will lead to such ill effects as boneache and sprains. Even after you have succeeded in leg suspending and leg splitting, you still have to practise in the exercises once every two or three days to prevent the retrogression of the ability obtained.

LEG SNAPPING

Leg snapping is also called "leg slipping" by masters of Chinese martial arts. It is an indispensable way for them to practise in leg training and strength transferring. So there goes the saying that "slip the feet out alternately thousands of times and the strength of the legs will certainly be transferred naturally". However, each school has different methods. In most cases, they have no systematic styles to follow. Even if some may have certain styles, they are merely random ones for casual kicking. I have compiled the methods of leg snapping and divided them into higher, medium and lower groups, each of which is in turn divided into four steps for training, that is to say, the total steps amount to twelve. The twelve steps also fall into three types: longer, medium and shorter types. Now let me illustrate them step by step as follows for the reference of those who are fond of leg striking:—

左腿擗畢，可繼如前法擗右腿。如是左右互練，至力盡為止。然後略做「曲膝蹲」數次，起立往來溜腿數十趟，使鬆活筋血，以免不調。

此法早晚各行功一次，可與吊腿法並行。普通未滿三十者，夏季一月，冬季月半，必然成功。成功之後，不但兩腿之筋肌堅強活軟，富有彈性，且高踢可至頂（高踢過頂者，非真軟腿，不可不知），下臥可貼地。然練腿者，切戒好勝心。若速求成功，致有脈骨疼痛，及扭筋傷氣之虞。至吊腿及擗腿已經成功者，尚需每隔二三日行功一次，以防功退。

踢 腿 法

踢腿者，乃武術家所謂之「溜腿」，為武術家練腿貫勁不可少之門徑，所謂「溜腿千百遍，腿勁必自然」也。然其法各家不同，多無系統架式可循，有者亦二三散式踢踢而已。余編有練腿之法，踢腿分上中下三盤，每盤分四趟練習，共十二趟。十二趟練法中，又分長中短三種腿法。茲分趟圖解如次，俾有志腿擊者參考：

下盤腿第一趟——正蹴腿

此趟，乃為練習足尖點勁之法。

先兩拳抱腰，立正，目向前視。

承上式，上左步，同時施彈勁，向前擊右拳。見第七圖。

承上式，將重心移於左前步，略提右腿。

承上式，左步略曲，身向下坐，蓄勁於右足尖，配合右使勁回收之勢；左拳右腳施彈勁向前發出。見第八圖。

THE 1ST STEP OF LOWER SNAPPING — FORWARD KICK

This step is a method of training in the pushing force of the tip of a foot.

Stand upright akimbo with both fists clenched, looking to the front.

· Following the preceding posture, move the left foot a step forward, exerting an elastic force, and rush the right fist forward. See Fig. 7.

Following the preceding movement, shift the centre of gravity onto the left foot and lift the right leg a little.

Following the preceding movement, bend the left leg a little, lower the body and transfer strength onto the tip of the right foot so as to support the right foot in its exertion of force and its drawing back; rush the left fist and snap the right foot forward, exerting an elastic force. See Fig. 8.

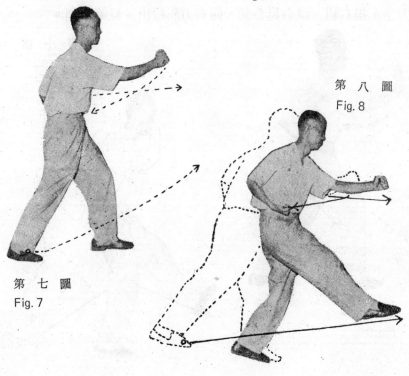

第 八 圖
Fig. 8

第 七 圖
Fig. 7

23

承上式，右腳蹬盡，落地成右弓步，是爲正蹬腿之右式；右式蹬完，再蹬左式。如是一左一右，連環踢腿，不計次數，至勁將盡，可繼踢第二趟。久之勁力自貫腳尖，然練時定要一氣呵成，不可分段練習。

下盤腿第二趟——正採腿

此趟，乃爲練習蹬訣斜勁之法。

承第一趟正蹬腿右式至盡，右足落地，穩定重心，配合身向左後轉之勢，使勁收回左拳，同時發擊右掌。見第九圖。

承上式，右掌向前擊出將盡，即向右下方如拉物狀，向右下挫拉；同時配合右手向右下挫拉之勢，重心移於左步，身向下坐，提右腿，以右足心勁，向右方斜蹬出。見第十圖。

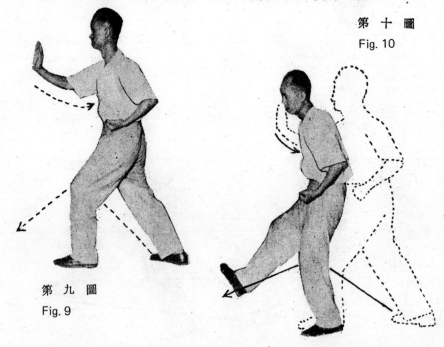

第 十 圖
Fig. 10

第 九 圖
Fig. 9

24

Following the preceding movement, after the right foot goes as far as it can, drop it on the ground and bow the leg forward. This is the right mode of the Forward Kick; after carrying out the right mode, practise in the left one. Doing the exercise alternately in this way, kicking countless times in a running way until the feet are about to be exhausted. Then go on with the 2nd step. As time passes, your strength will naturally be transferred to the tips of your feet. But the exercise must be done at a stretch without any intervals.

THE 2ND STEP OF LOWER SNAPPING — SLANTING KICK

This step is a method of training in the exertion of a slanting force in the trick of Straight Kicking.

Following the end of the right mode of the 1st step (Forward Kick), drop the right foot on the ground, making the centre of gravity steady and turning the body left to the back; draw the left fist back forcefully and rush the right palm out at the same time. See Fig. 9.

Following the preceding movement, after the right palm goes nearly as far as it can, drop it and draw it to the right lower side as if pulling something; in coordination with this movement, shift the centre of gravity onto the left foot, lower the body, lift the right leg up and snap the foot slantingly out to the right side with the force of the right sole. See Fig. 10.

Following the preceding movement, drop the right foot on the ground and bow the leg forward; draw the right fist back and rush the left palm out forcefully at the same time. See the left mode in Fig. 9, which is the right mode of the Slanting Kick.

Following the preceding movement, after carrying out the right mode, go on with the left one in the same way. Do these running alternate exercises countless times in this way until your feet are about to be exhausted. Then go on with the 3rd step. As time passes, your strength will naturally be transferred onto the soles.

承上式，右足蹬畢，落地成右弓步，同時施勁收回右拳，而發左掌。如第九圖之左式。是爲正探腿之右式。

承上式，正探腿之右式探畢，再繼而依法探蹬左式。如是一左一右，連環探蹬，不計其數，至勁將盡，可繼而踢第三趟，久之勁力自貫足心。

下盤腿第三趟──鈎掃腿

此趟，乃爲練習鈎、掃二訣直勁之法。

承第二趟正探腿右式至盡，配合身向左轉後之勢，收左掌至腿際，同時提右腿，運勁至右脚之前脛部，向前鈎掃自己左脚之後脛部（右脚鈎掃時，左脚須迎力施勁站穩，否則可能將自己鈎倒）。見第十一圖。

承上式，右足鈎掃畢，向前開一步，成右弓步式，是爲鈎掃腿之右式。

承上式，立穩重心，再以左脚如右式法，向前鈎掃自己右脚後脛，是爲鈎掃腿之左式。

承上式，左式練畢，繼練右式。如是一左一右，向前連環鈎掃，不計其數，久之勁力自貫脚脛。

第十一圖　Fig. 11

THE 3RD STEP OF LOWER SNAPPING —
HOOKING & SWEEPING

This step is a method of training in the exertion of a straight force in the two tricks of hooking and sweeping.

Following the end of the right mode of the Slanting Kick, turning the body left to the back, draw the left palm back to the lateral side of the left leg; at the same time, lift the right leg up backward, transfer your strength onto the front of the right shin and use the part to hook and sweep the back of your own left shin forward (when the right foot is hooking and sweeping, the left foot should keep steady forcefully against the coming force, otherwise you may be tripped up by yourself). See Fig. 11.

Following the preceding movement, move the right foot a step forward and bow the leg forward. This is the right mode of Hooking and Sweeping.

Following the preceding movement, stand with the centre of gravity kept steady and go on with the left foot in the same way as in the right mode, i.e. hook and sweep the back of your own right shin forward with the front of the left shin. This is the right mode of Hooking and Sweeping.

Following the preceding movement, after carrying out the left mode, go on with the right one. Train alternately in this way in the left and right modes, hooking and sweeping forward countless times in a running way. As time passes, your strength will naturally be transferred onto the feet and shins.

THE 4TH STEP OF LOWER SNAPPING —
CIRCLING AND BACK-SNAPPING

This way is a method of training in the exertion of a slanting force in the trick of Snapping.

Following the end of the right mode of the 3rd step (Hooking & Sweeping), turning the body left to the back, shift the centre of gravity onto the left foot and bow the leg forward; at the

下盤腿第四類趟——圈彈腿

此趟，乃爲練習彈訣斜勁之法。

承上第三趟鈎掃腿之右式至盡，配合身向左轉後之勢，重心移於左步，成左弓步式，同時曲右膝，以右小腿勁向前下點蹴（此爲虛着）。見第十二圖。

承上式，右足點蹴將盡，即配合身向左後轉之勢，右腿向左方轉圈形，以足後跟向上施勁反彈（此爲實着）。見第十三圖。

承上式，右足反彈至盡，身向右後轉，同時右足落地，成右弓步式，是爲圈彈腿之右式。

承上式，右式圈腿彈畢，再繼圈彈左式，如是一左一右，連環圈彈，不計其數，久之勁力自貫脚尖及足跟。

第 十 二 圖
Fig. 12

28

same time, bend the right knee and strike the foot down to the front with the force of the right shin (this is a false movement). See Fig. 12.

Following the preceding movement, after the right foot nearly goes as far as it can, turning the body left to the back, circle the right foot to the left and snap it backward forcefully with the heel facing upward (this is a real movement). See Fig. 13.

Following the preceding movement, after the right foot goes as far as it can, turn the body right to the back; at the same time, drop the right foot on the ground and bow the leg forward. This is the right mode of Circling & Backsnapping.

Following the preceding movement, after carrying out the right mode, go on with the left one. Train alternately in this way, circling and back-snapping countless times in a running way. As time passes, your strength can naturally be transferred onto the tips of the feet and heels.

第十三圖

Fig. 13

中盤腿第一趟——鴛奮腿

此趟，乃爲練習點、蹬二訣橫斜勁之法。

先面北抱拳立正，沉氣靜神，後上右步，施彈勁向前擊左掌。見第十四圖。

承上式，重心移於左步，身向右前方轉動，面向東，虛吊右步，雙掌如捧物狀於胸前，掌心向上，勢如「美如照鏡」。見第十五圖。

承上式，左步略曲，身向下坐，蓄勁於右足尖，配合雙掌向南撥擊之勢，右足尖施彈勁向南點蹴。見第十六圖。

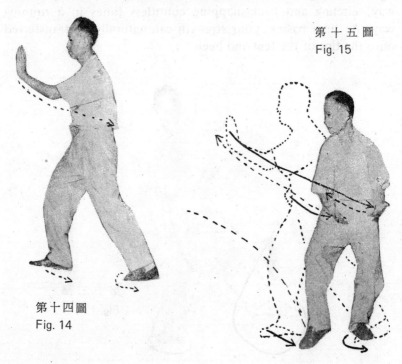

第十五圖
Fig. 15

第十四圖
Fig. 14

THE 1ST STEP OF MEDIUM SNAPPING — COUPLE KICKS

This step is a method of training in the exertion of a transverse or slanting force in the two tricks of Shoving and Straight-kicking.

First stand upright with the fists clenched, facing north, and calm your mind; then move the right foot a step forward and rush the left palm forward, exerting an elastic force. See Fig. 14.

Following the preceding movement, shift the centre of gravity onto the left foot and turn the body to the right front to face east and lift the right heel up to touch the ground only with the tip of the foot, both palms facing upward in front of the chest as if holding something or as looking in a mirror like a beauty. See Fig. 15.

Following the preceding movement, bend the left leg a little, lower the body and transfer your strength onto the tip of the right foot; rushing both palms to the south, snap the tip of the right foot to the south, exerting an elastic force. See Fig. 16.

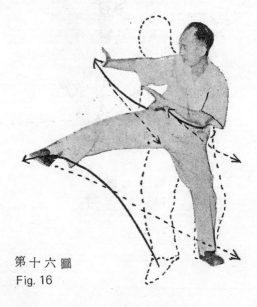

第十六圖
Fig. 16

承上式，右足點盡，即施彈勁收回，由左步前置左步之左側，左步隨勢提起，同時雙手向左下捋。見第十七圖。

承上式，左步一提起，向北退一步，身向右轉，面向南，右掌向上挑，左掌置右肘底下；同時右步虛吊，成南向右避掌式。見第十八圖。是為右鴛鴦腿。

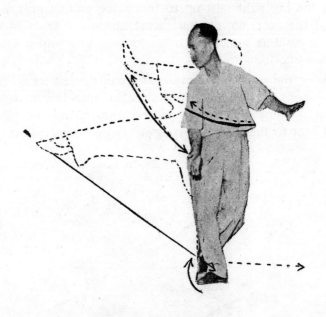

第 十 七 圖

Fig. 17

Following the preceding movement, after the right foot goes as far as it can, draw it back, exerting an elastic force and putting it on the left of the left foot passing by the front of the left foot; correspondingly, lift the left foot up; at the same time, throw both hands down to the left. See Fig. 17.

Following the preceding movement, as soon as the left foot is lifted up, draw it a step back to the north and turn the body to the right to face north; pick the right palm up and place the left one under the right elbow; at the same time, lift the right heel up to touch the ground only with the tip of the foot. See Fig. 18. This is the right mode of the Couple Kicks.

Following the preceding movement, when drawing the right foot back, thread the left palm forward from under the right elbow and draw the right palm back. See Fig. 19.

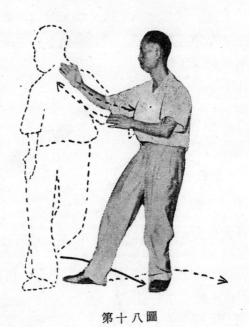

第十八圖

Fig. 18

承上式，左掌配合右步向後退之勢，由右肘底向前穿，右掌向回縮，成左避掌式。見第十九圖。

承上式，左掌揮盡，即向回收，重心移於右步，雙掌掌心向上如捧物狀於胸前，勢如美女照鏡，同時虛吊左步。如第十五圖之左式。

承上式，右步略曲，身向下坐，蓄勁於左足尖，配合雙掌向南撥擊之勢，左足尖施彈勁向南蹴點。如第十六圖之左式。

承上式，左足點蹴盡，即施彈勁收回，由右步前置於右步之右側，右步隨勢提起，同時雙手向右下摔。如第十七圖之左式。

承上式，右步一提起，向北退一步，身向左轉，面向南，左掌向上挑，右掌置左肘底下，同時虛吊左步，成南向左避掌式。是爲左鴛鴦腿。如第十八圖之左式。

承上式，左鴛鴦腿練完，再繼蹴右鴛鴦腿，如是一左一右，連環點蹴，不計次數，久之勁力自貫足尖。

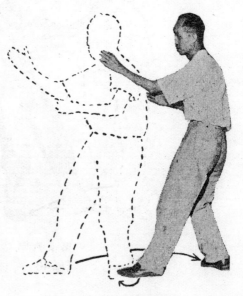

第十九圖
Fig. 19

Following the preceding movement, after the left palm goes as far as it can, draw it back and shift the centre of gravity onto the right foot, both palms facing upward in front of the chest as if holding something or looking in the mirrow like a beauty; ast the same time, lift the left heel up to touch the ground with the tip of the foot as in the left mode of Fig. 15.

Following the preceding movement, bend the right leg a little, lower the body and transfer your strength onto the tip of the left foot; rushing both palms to tbe south, snap the tip of your left foot to the south, exerting an elastic force. See the left mode of Fig. 16.

Following the preceding movement, after the left foot goes as far as it can, draw it back with an elastic force and put it on the right of the right foot, passing by the front of the right leg; correspondingly, lift the right foot up; at the same time, throw both hands down to the right as in the left mode of Fig. 17.

Following the preceding movement, as soon as the right foot is lifted up, draw it a step back to the north and turn the body left to face south; pick the left palm up and put the right palm under the left elbow; at the same time, lift the left heel up to touch the ground only with the tip of the foot. This is the left mode of the Couple Kicks, as in the left mode of Fig. 18.

Following the preceding movement, after carrying out the left mode of the Couple Kicks, go on with the right mode. Train in this way alternately in the left and right modes, striking countless times in a running way. As time passes, your strength can naturally be transferred onto the tips of the feet.

THE 2ND STEP OF MEDIUM SNAPPING — TRANSVERSE STRAIGHT KICK

This step is a method of training in the exertion of a straight or transverse force in the trick of Straight-kicking.

Following the end of the right mode of the 1st step (Couple Kicks), move the slightly lifted right foot half a step forward and bow the leg forward; draw the right palm back and rush the left one forward.

中盤腿第二趟——橫蹬腿

此趟，乃為練習蹬訣橫直勁之法。

承上第一趟至右避掌式時，將虛吊之右步，向前踏半步，成右弓左箭步，收回右掌向前擊出左掌。

承上式左掌向上向前穿出，同時配合穿左掌之勢，身略下坐，勁貫左足心，身略右轉，左足施彈勁，向前橫蹬，高與胸齊。見第二十圖。

承上式，左足蹬畢，向前向下踏，成左弓步，同時左掌向前按擊，至此是為左蹬腿。見第二十一圖。

承上式，左掌按勁將盡，即向回收，同時右掌由左肘下向上向前穿，同時配合右掌前穿之勢，身向左轉，重心穩於左步，勁貫右足心，施彈勁向前橫蹬，高與胸齊。如第二十圖之右式。

承上式，右足蹬畢，向前向下踏，成右弓步，同時右掌向前按擊，至此是為右蹬腿。

如第二十一圖之右式。

承上式，右腿蹬畢，繼蹬左腿。如是一左一右，連環橫蹬，不計其數，久之勁力自貫足心。

第二十圖

Fig. 20

36

Following the preceding movement, thread the left palm out upward and forward; at the same time, lower the body slightly and transfer your strength onto the sole of the left foot; turning the body right a little, snap the left foot transversely forward up to the height of the chest, exerting an elastic force. See Fig. 20.

Following the preceding movement, after the left ·foot goes as far as it can, stamp it down forward and bow the leg forward; at the same time, oush the left palm forward. This is the left mode of the Transverse Straight Kick. See Fig. 21.

Following the preceding movement, after the left palm goes nearly as far as it can, draw it back; at the same time, thread the right palm upward and forward from under the left elbow; in coordination with this, turn the body left, keeping the centre of gravity steady on the left foot; transfer your strength onto the sole of the right foot and snap it transversely forward up to the height of the chest, exerting an elastic force, as in the right mode of Fig. 20.

Following the preceding movement, after the right foot goes as far as it can, stamp it down forward and bow the leg forward; at the same time, push the right palm forward. This is the right mode of the Transverse Straight Kick, as in the right mode of Fig. 21.

Following the preceding movement, after the right mode is over, go on with the left one. Train in this way alternately in the left and right modes, snapping transversely countless times in a running way. As time passes, your strength can naturally be transferred onto the soles of the feet.

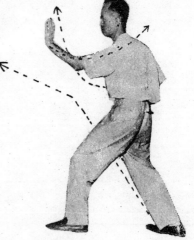

第二十一圖

Fig. 21

中盤腿第三趟──穿心腿

此趟，乃為練習足跟蹬訣直上勁之法。

承上第二趟右蹬腿畢，向後轉身，成左弓步，將重心移於左步，配合雙手向上向左右分撥之勢，身略下坐，蓄勁於右足後跟，施彈勁由胸前，向上向前蹬出，高過胸口。見第二十二圖。

承上式，右足蹬畢，向下踏落，成右弓步；同時雙手亦向下撲，交叉於腹部。至此是為右穿心腿。

承上式，右腿蹬畢，再繼而蹬左穿心腿。如是一左一右，連環穿蹬，不計其數，久之勁力自貫足跟。

第二十二圖

Fig. 22

38

THE 3RD STEP OF MEDIUM SNAPPING —
HEART-HITTING KICK

This step is a method of training in the exertion of a straight or upward force in the trick of Straight-kicking with a heel.

Following the end of the right mode of the Transverse Straight Kick (the 2nd step), turn the body back and bow the left leg forward, shifting the centre of gravity onto the left foot; parting both hands upward to both sides, lower the body slightly, transfer strength onto the right heel and make it kick out upward and forward higher than the chest from front of the chest, exerting an elastic force. See Fig. 22.

Following the preceding movement, after the right foot goes as far as it can, drop it on the ground and bow the leg forward; at the same time, throw both hands down and cross them in front of the abdomen. This is the right mode of the Heart-hitting Kick.

Following the preceding movement, after carrying out the right mode, go on with the left mode. Train in these alternate running hitting kicks countless times. As time passes, your strength can naturally be transferred onto the heels.

THE 4TH STEP OF MEDIUM SNAPPING —
SLANTING SNAPPING

This step is a method of training in the exertion of a slanting force in the trick of Bumping or the trick of Straight-kicking.

Following the end of the right mode of the 3rd step the Heart-hitting Kick, turn the body left to the back, and in coordination with this movement, sink the body a little, transfer strength onto the right knee and rush it to the left front side, exerting an elastic force. See Fig. 23.

Following the preceding movement, after the right knee goes slantingly nearly as far as it can, transfer strength onto the right sole and snap it slantingly to the right lower side. See Fig. 24.

Following the preceding movement, after the right foot

中盤腿第四趟——斜彈腿

此趟，乃爲練習撞訣斜勁，及登訣斜勁之法。

承上第三趟穿心腿右蹬腿畢，身向左後轉，同時配合轉身之勢，身略下沉，蓄勁於右膝頭，施彈勁向左前方撞去。見第二十三圖。

承上式，右膝斜撞將盡，即貫勁右足心，向右下斜斜彈蹬。見第二十四圖。

承上式，右足彈蹬畢，即翻落成右弓步，是爲斜彈右式。

承上式，右式練畢，將重心穩於右步，配合身向上抽之勢，蓄勁於左膝頭，施彈勁向左方撞去。如第二十三圖之左式。

承上式，左膝斜撞將盡，即貫勁左足心，向右下斜斜彈蹬，如第二十四圖之左式。然後翻落成左弓步，是爲斜彈腿之左式。

承上式，左式彈蹬畢，再繼而彈蹬右式。如是一左一右，連環彈蹬，不計其數，久之勁力自貫於膝頭足心。

第二十三圖
Fig. 23

goes as far as it can, drop it on the ground and bow the leg forward. This is the right mode of Slanting Snapping.

Following the preceding movement, after the right mode is completed, keep the centre of gravity steady on the right foot; jerking the body up, transfer strength onto the left knee and rush it to the left side, exerting an elastic force, as in the left mode of Fig. 23.

Following the preceding movement, after the left knee goes slantingly nearly as far as it can, transfer strength onto the left sole and snap it slantingly to the right lower side as the left mode of Fig. 24. Then drop it on the ground and bow the leg forward. This is the left mode of Slanting Snapping.

Following the preceding movement, after the left mode is completed, go on with the right one. Train in these alternate running kicks in this way countless times. As time passes, your strength can naturally be transferred onto the knees and soles.

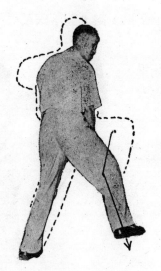

第二十四圖
Fig. 24

41

上盤腿第一趟——上踢腿

此趟，乃爲練習點訣上勁之法。

承上中盤腿法第四趟右式畢，身向左後轉，同時乘身向後轉之勢，將重心移於左步，身略下坐，蓄勁於腰際，貫勁於右足尖，左手向後鈎，右掌上翻，以右足尖向上向己踢點右掌心。見第二十五圖。

承上式，右足上踢腿，向下翻落成右弓步，順勢向前按擊右掌。是爲右式。

承上式，右掌按勁將盡，左鈎手變掌，掌心向上，由右掌上穿過，而向上翻；右掌則變鈎手，鈎於後。同時左脚配合左掌向上翻，右掌向後鈎之勢，身略下坐，重心移於右步，施彈勁向上向己以脚尖踢左掌心。如二十五圖之左式。

承上式，左足上踢畢，向下翻落成左弓步，順勢向前按擊左掌，是爲左式。

承上式，左式踢畢，再繼之右式。如是一左一右，連環不息，久之勁力自貫足尖及掌心。

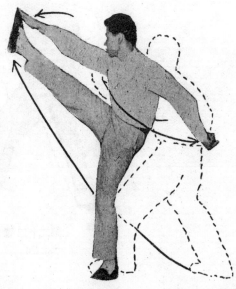

第二十五圖
Fig. 25

THE 1ST STEP OF HIGHER SNAPPING — UPWARD KICK

This step is a method of training in the exertion of an upward force in the trick of Shoving.

Following the end of the right mode of Medium Snapping, turn the body left to the back; at the same time, shift the centre of gravity accordingly onto the left foot, lower the body a little, concentrate strength between the loins and then transfer it onto the tip of the right foot; hook the left hand backward, turn the right palm over and snap the tip of the right foot upward against the right palm. See Fig. 25.

Following the preceding movement, after the right foot hits the palm, drop it on the ground and bow the leg forward and push the right palm forward accordingly. This is the right mode.

Following the preceding movement, after the right palm goes nearly as far as it can, turn the left hooked hand into a flat palm, facing upward, thread it over the right palm and turn it over; turn the right palm into a hooked hand and place it behind the body. At the same time, in coordination with these movements, lower the body a little, shift the centre of gravity onto the right foot and snap the tip of the left foot upward against the left palm, exerting an elastic force, as the left mode of Fig. 25.

Following the preceding movement, after the left foot hits the left palm, drop it on the ground and bow the leg forward, and push the left palm forward accordingly. This is the left mode.

Following the preceding movement, after the left mode is completed, go on with the right one. Train in these alternate running movements continuously in this way. As time passes, your strength can naturally be transferred onto the palms and the tips of the feet.

上盤腿第二趟——連環腿

此趟，乃爲練習輕身，及點訣直彈勁之法。

承上第一趟上踢右腿畢，順勢上左步擊左掌。見第二十六圖虛線A。

承上式，重心移於右步，趁身向下一坐之勢，氣向上提，將身向上凌空提起，右掌回收，右脚凌空向前點蹴而向上挑，同時以右掌迎拍左脚面襪勢。見第二十六圖黑線B。

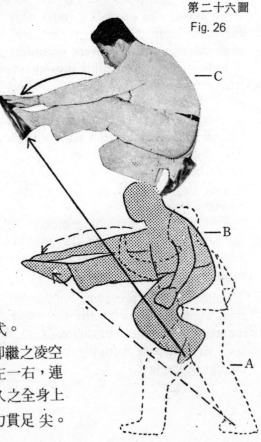

第二十六圖
Fig. 26

承上式，右足點蹴將盡，即向回彈收，凌空配合右掌右足回收之勢，以左足向前點蹴而向上挑，同時左掌拍左脚面襪勢。見第二十六圖之C。

承上式，左足點蹴將畢，即落右步，隨落左步。待左步一落穩，收回左掌，上右步，發右掌。至此是爲右連環腿。如第二十六圖虛線A之左式。

承上右式蹴畢，即繼之凌空連環蹴左式。如是一左一右，連環飛蹴，不計其數，久之全身上提下落輕捷無聲，勁力貫足尖。

THE 2ND STEO OF HIGHER SNAPPING — RUNNING KICKS

This step is a method of training in getting the body light and in the exertion of a straight force in the trick of Shoving.

Following the end of the right mode of the 1st step (Upward Kick), move the left foot forward and rush the left palm out accordingly. See the dotted line A in Fig. 26.

Following the preceding movement, shift the centre of gravity onto the right foot, and in coordination with the lowering of the body, raise your strength and spring up into the air; draw the right palm back and snap the right foot forward and pick it up in the air, clapping the right palm against the face of the right foot. See the dotted lines B in Fig. 26.

Following the preceding movement, after the right foot goes up nearly as far as it can, snap it back in the air; in coordination with this movement, snap the left foot forward and pick it up, clapping the left palm against the face of the left foot. See C in Fig. 26.

Following the preceding movement, after the left fot goes up as far as it can, drop the right foot and then the left one on the ground; as soon as the left foot gets steady, draw the left palm back, move the right foot forward and rush the right palm out. This is the right mode of the Running Kicks, as the left mode of the dotted lines A in Fig. 26.

Following the preceding movement, after the right mode is completed, go on with the left one of the Running Kicks in the air. Train in this way in the left and right modes, kicking in a running way countless times. As time passes, the body can become so light that there is no noise when jerking it up and dropping it and your strength can be transferred onto the tips of the feet.

THE 3RD STEP OF HIGHER SNAPPING — FLYING AND CUTTING

This step is a method of training in the exertion of a straight upward force in the trick of cutting with the lateral sides of the

上盤腿第三趟——飛割腿

此趟，乃為練習足部外側割訣直上勁之法。

承上第二趟連環腿右式蹴畢，先將重心移於左步，氣向下沉，左腿略曲，配合上身向後仰之勢，貫勁於右足部外側，由下向上向外割，如以刀向上向前劏之意。見第二十七圖。

承上式，右足割畢，輕輕落地成右弓步，是為飛割腿之右式。

承上式，右式割畢，再繼以左式。如是一左一右連環飛割，不計其數，久之勁力自貫足緣。

按：割腿與身勢，動作要襯合，如蛇之首尾相應，方為上乘。

第二十七圖

Fig. 27

46

feet.

Following the end of the right mode of the 2nd step the Running Kicks, shift the centre of gravity onto the left foot, sink strength and bend the left leg slightly; leaning the upper body backward, transfer strength to the lateral side of the right foot and make it cut upward and outward from below like using a knife. See Fig. 27.

Following the preceding movement, after the right foot goes as far as it can, drop it gently on the ground and bow the leg forward. This is the right mode of Flying and Cutting.

following the preceding movement, after the right mode is completed, go on with the left one. Train alternately in this way, flying and cutting countless times in a trunning way. As time passes, your strength can naturally be transferred onto the lateral sides of the feet.

It is excellent to get the movements of the feet coordinated with those of the body just like the head and tail of a snake.

THE 4TH STEP OF HIGHER SNAPPING — BOTH FEET FLYING

This step is a method of training in getting the body light and in the exertion of a straight force in the trick of Shoving.

Following the end of the right mode of the 3rd step (Flying & Cutting), move the left foot forward accordingly and bring it close to the right one; bending both knees slightly, rush both palms forward. See Fig. 28.

Following the preceding movement, lower the body, snap the tips of both feet against the ground, exerting an elastic force, and accordingly, raising both hands and heaving strength, spring up into the air; at this moment, snap both feet forward and pick them up; at the same time, clap both palms down against the faces of the feet. See Fig. 29.

Following the preceding movement, after both feet are flown up, sink strength and drop the body with the tips of the feet touching the ground to avoid any sound; at the same time, drop both palms. See Fig. 28.

上盤腿第四趟——雙飛腿

此趟，乃爲練習輕身，及點訣直勁之法。

承上第三趟飛割腿右式畢，順勢上左步與右步相併，雙膝略曲，同時向前擊雙掌。見第二十八圖。

承上式，身向下坐，雙足尖使彈勁向地蹬，順勢雙手上揚，氣向上提，身向上凌空。即乘全身凌空之際，雙足齊向前蹴而向上挑；同時雙掌向下拍雙足面襯勢。見第二十九圖。

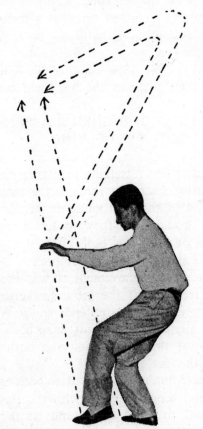

第二十八圖
Fig. 28

48

Following the preceding movement, after both feet reach the ground, snap the tips of the feet once more against the ground, and heaving strength up and raise both hands, spring up into the air and snap both feet up forward. Train in this way like an eagle, rising and dropping countless times in a running way. As time passes, your body will become as light as a swallow and your strength can be transferred onto the tips of the feet.

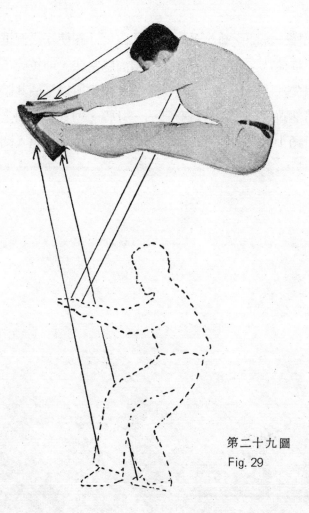

第二十九圖
Fig. 29

承上式，雙足蹴畢，氣向下沉，身向下落，雙足以足尖落地，勿使有聲，雙掌亦同時下放。見第二十八圖。

承上式，雙足一着地，即以足尖向地一蹬，配合氣向上提，雙手向上揚之勢，再繼之凌空雙足一齊飛蹴。如是一起一落，勢若旋鷹，連環飛擊，不計其數，久之身自輕如燕，而勁力貫足尖。

按：練腿之難，果安在哉？曰：「在使腿法沉重與輕快二點並進而已。」上述三盤十二趟溜腿之法，即按此二要點而編之；先練下盤所以屹立其身，終練上盤所以靈活其體也。果能按路熟習苦練，久之自有腳活、身輕、勁貫、氣順之效。如繼之研通十三訣，運之二十四法，腳擊之道，可謂入門矣。

Does any difficulty exist in leg training? The answer is that leg training is only for the purpose to make the feet strike both heavily and gently at will. The compilation of the above-mentioned twelve steps in three groups is based on the two main purposes. First train in lower snapping so as to make the body stand steadily and then train in higher snapping to make free the body. If you really train in accordance with the methods and insist on it, you can obtain the effects of lively feet movement, light body, free strength transfer and smooth respiration. If you go on with the exercises in the thirteen tricks and proceed to the twenty four techniques, you can be said to have crossed the threshold of the methods of foot striking.

腿法十三訣

我國武術之腿擊，乃係指腿足之全部運用而言，如跨、膝、足、脛、踵等，均含其內。吾編之各家腿法精華，有十三訣，以十三字示之，即點、蹬、割、擦、彈、絆、挑、鈎、掃、剪、跺、撞、挾也。茲釋其要義如下：

點 點者，踢也。以足掌前部向前踢敵中下盤之法。見第三十圖之A。

蹬 蹬者，撐也。以踵(足後跟)前蹬後撐敵中上盤之法。見第三十圖之B。

割 割者，剷也。以足掌外緣，橫割敵下盤，及上剷敵喉部之法。見第三十圖之C。

擦 擦者，剷也。以足掌外緣，直下剷敵下盤小腿上下五寸之法。見第三十圖之C。

彈 彈者，崩也。以足踵反彈敵下陰、肘、腕等部之法。見第三十圖之D。

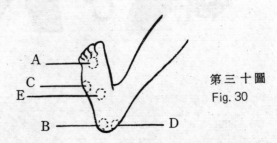

第三十圖
Fig. 30

THIRTEEN FOOT STRIKING
TRICKS

The foot striking in Chinese martial arts refers to the use of all the parts of the legs and feet, such as thighs, knees, feet, shins, heels, etc., which are all included. The essences of the foot striking techniques of every school compiled by me contain thirteen tricks which I have designated as thirteen words, i.e. shoving, straight-kicking, cutting, shaving, snapping, tripping, picking, hooking, sweeping, clipping, stamping, bumping and clamping. Now let me explain their main definitions as follows:—

Shoving is also known as kicking, which is to kick forward at the medium and lower parts of an opponent with the front parts of the soles. See A in Fig. 30.

Straight-Kicking is also known as punting, which is to kick forward and punt backward against the medium and lower parts of an opponent with the heels. See B in Fig. 30.

Cutting is also known as chopping, which is to cut the lower part of an opponent transversely with the lateral side of a foot or to cut the opponent's throat with it. See C in Fig. 30.

Shaving is also known as scraping, which is to cut the upper and lower parts of an opponent's shank with the lateral side of a foot. See C in Fig. 30.

Snapping is also known as jerking, which is to snap a heel backward against private part, elbow, wrist, etc. of an opponent. See D in Fig. 30.

Tripping is also known as felling, which is to fell an opponent by tripping up his lower part with a shank. See A and D in Fig. 31.

Picking is also known as scooping, which is to pick the face of

絆　絆者，別也。以小腿別敵下盤使跌之法。見第三十一圖之Ａ及Ｄ。

挑　挑者，撩也。以足面向上挑擊敵下陰或手肘等部之法。見第三十一圖之Ｂ。

鈎　鈎者，帶也，以足脛鈎敵下盤使跌之法。見第三十一圖之Ａ及Ｃ。

掃　掃者，撥也。以足脛掃敵下盤使跌之法。見第三十一圖之Ｃ。

剪　剪者，迎也。以兩腿之迎面骨及腿肚子，剪敵中下盤之法。見第三十一圖之Ｄ及Ｅ。

踩　踩者，踏也。以足心向下踏敵之法。見第三十圖之Ｅ及Ｂ。

撞　撞者，碰也。以胯或膝向上或向前撞敵中下盤之法。見第三十一圖之Ｇ。

挾　挾者，迫也。以兩膝閃側，迎合兩足鈎勁挾敵腰胸之法。見第三十一圖之Ｆ。

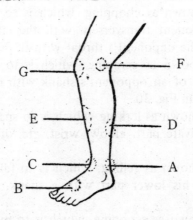

第三十一圖
Fig. 31

54

a foot up to strike at an opponent's parts, such as his private part, hand, elbow, etc.. See B in Fig. 31.

Hooking is also known as carrying, which is to fell an opponent by hooking his lower part with a shin. See A and C in Fig. 31.

Sweeping is also known as poking, which is to fell an opponent by sweeping his lower part with a shin. See C in Fig. 31.

Clipping is also known as meeting, which is to clip an opponent's medium and lower parts with a tibia of one leg and a calf of the other leg. See D and E in Fig. 31.

Stamping is also known as tramping, which is to kick down against an opponent's foot with a sole. See E and B in Fig. 30.

Bumping is also known as knocking, which is to knock at an opponent's medium and lower parts with a thigh or knee moving upward or forward. See G in Fig. 31.

Clamping is also known as pressing, which is to clamp an opponent's chest and waist by parting both knees and then clamping with the force of the hooking of the feet. See F in Fig. 31.

腿擊要害部位

腿法十三訣，所取人體要害，分三盤，輕取可使傷，重取可即喪命。三盤者，心窩以上各部，為上盤。下陰以上各部，為中盤。足部以上各部，為下盤。三盤要害部位圖解如下：

正面（見第三十二圖）

上盤：1.喉　2.乳　3.心窩　4.腋　5.肘　6.腕　7.脇

中盤：1.丹田　2.胯　3.下陰　4.腰軟　5.胃

下盤：

1.膝節
2.踝
3.足背
4.脛
5.迎面骨

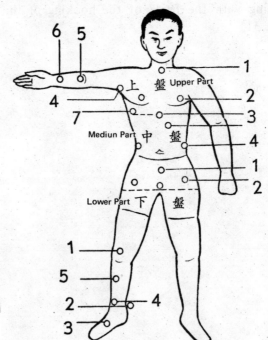

第三十二圖
Fig. 32

56

THE VITAL PARTS FOR
FOOT STRIKING

The vital parts of a human body which the thirteen foot striking tricks aim at are divided into three parts. Hitting gently may hurt a person and hitting heavily may kill him or her at once. The three parts are as follows: the parts above the cavity of stomach are included in the upper part; the parts above the private part and below the navel are included in the medium part; and the parts above the feet and below the hip are included in the lower part. Now illustrate the vital parts in these three parts as follows:—

Front (See Fig. 32)

Upper Part: 1. throat, 2. breasts, 3. the cavity of stomach, 4. armpits, 5. elbows, 6. wrists and 7. ribs

Medium Part: 1. navel, 2. hip, 3. private part, 4. loins and 5. stomach

Lower Part: 1. knees, 2. ankles, 3. the backs of feet, 4. shins and 5. tibiae

背面（見第三十三圖）

上盤：1.對心　2.肘

中盤：1.軟腰　2.尾龍骨

下盤：1.膝彎　2.踁

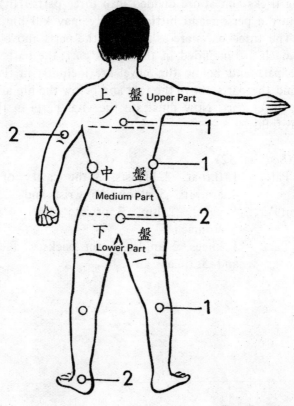

第三十三圖

Fig. 33

Back (See Fig. 33)

Upper Part: 1. heart location and 2. elbows

Medium Part: 1. loins and 2. coccyx

Lower Part: 1. the hollows of the knees and 2. shins

二十四腿法

第一法——蹬膝腿

此法乃乘敵一拳擊來時，巧蹬其膝節，折之或挫之之法。

圖解：設敵突然一拳擊來，我即乘其衝來之勢，身略向左側閃，避過其右拳。隨即右手翻上，將敵擊來之右手腕抓住。見第三十四圖，圖中A爲敵方，B爲我方。下同。

承上式，我一將敵右腕抓住，即配合右腳施蹬訣直勁，向敵右前膝節蹬去之勢；右手緊握敵右腕，向我右後方猛拉。見第三十五圖。

按：敵在此一拉一蹬之間，必魄散神昏，其右膝即不折，亦必影響其攻勢。是時乘隙反攻，無有不克矣。

第三十四圖
Fig. 34

B

A

TWENTY—FOUR FOOT
STRIKING TECHNIQUES

TECHNIQUE 1 – KNEE-HITTING KICK

This technique is to strike skilfully at an opponent's knee in order to break or hurt it at the moment he (A) is giving me (B) a blow with one fist.

ILLUSTRATIONS: Supposing the opponent is giving me a sudden blow with one fist, I move my body accordingly a little to the left to dodge his right fist, then I turn my right hand upward and seize the coming right wrist of the opponent. See Fig. 34. In the figure, A is the opponent, B is the demonstrator (the same hereinafter).

Following the preceding movement, as soon as I seize the opponent's right wrist, I jerk my right foot at the opponent's right knee, exerting a straight force in the trick of Straight-kicking; grasping the opponent's right wrist firmly with my right hand, pull it forcefully to my right backside. See Fig. 35. The kicking and pulling will surely scare the opponent out of his wits. Even though his knee is not broken, his offensive will certainly be affected. I shall defeat him without exception if I

第三十五圖

Fig. 35

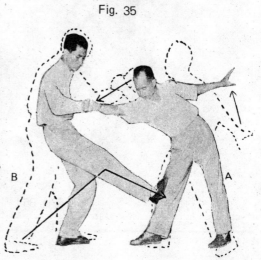

第二法——挑腿

此法乃係與敵爭執間，我突施之而取其命之法。

圖解：設我與敵爭執間，見敵不可理喻，而又非即施毒招不能自救時，即乘隙虛以右掌向敵胸部擊去；敵見我右掌擊其胸部，必然順勢用左手向外格攔。見第三十六圖。

承上式，我見敵以左手向外格撥我右掌，即乘其向外撥勢，右臂順其勢向外走，同時配合身向後仰之勢，突以右腳施挑訣上彈勁，向敵下陰部，由下向上以足背挑擊。見第三十七圖。

按：此法不中則已，中則敵必踣地大號，而失却反抗力。

第三十六圖
Fig. 36

take advantage of ,his blunder and counter-attack him.

TECHNIQUE 2 — PICKING KICK

This technique is to be abruptly used to kill an opponent when I am disputing with him.

ILLUSTRATIONS: Supposing I am disputing with the opponent, if he is impervious to reason and it is impossible for me to save myself unless I use a fierce stroke, I take advantage of his blunder and make a false attack upon his chest with my right palm; when he sees my right palm approaching his chest, he will surely hold it back outward with his left hand accordingly. See Fig. 36.

Following the preceding movement, when I see the opponent holding my right palm back outward with his left hand, I take advantage of the opportunity and move my right arm outward accordingly; at the same time, leaning my body backward, I suddenly pick my right foot up, exerting an elastic force, and strike up at his private part from below with the back of the foot. See Fig. 37.

Nothing will happen if the foot does not hit the mark; but if it hits, the opponent will certainly fall forward onto the ground and wail loudly so that he will lose his resistance.

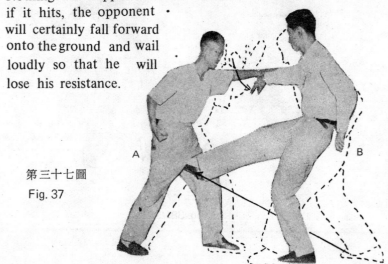

第三十七圖

Fig. 37

63

第三法——掃腿

此法乃係乘敵一拳擊來，或抓來之時，我突封其勢，而掃跌敵之法。

圖解：設我於不防備間，突被敵以右手抓住我胸部之衣，死纏不放，即乘其尚未施用其他手法謀我之前，身略向右轉，同時以右手將其抓我胸部之右手腕抓住。見第三十八圖。

承上式，我將敵右腕抓住，扣緊於胸前，順勢上左步於敵前步後方，同時配合左手向上伸，以小臂施勁對準敵之咽喉，向下向後撥格之勢，左腿施掃訣向前掃敵之步，則敵必喉傷而跌。見第三十九圖。

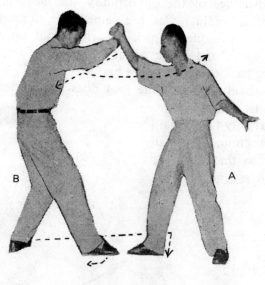

第三十八圖
Fig. 38

64

TECHNIQUE 3 – SWEEPING KICK

This technique is to suddenly block an opponent's attack and sweep his foot to fell him when he is giving me a blow with one fist or when he is seizing me.

ILLUSTRATIONS: Supposing I am seized off guard by my shirt in front of my chest by the opponent with his right hand and he keeps seizing, I take advantage of the chance before he uses other plots against me, and turning my body slightly to the right, seize his right wrist on my chest with my right hand. See Fig. 38.
Following the preceding movement, after I seize the opponent's right wrist, I press if firmly onto my chest and move my left foot forward accordingly to the backside of his front foot (i.e. the right foot in the illustration); stretching my left hand up and aiming my forearm, exerting a force, at his throat, poke it downward and backward and sweep the opponent's foot forward with my left leg. Then the opponent will surely get his throat hurt and fall down. See Fig. 39.

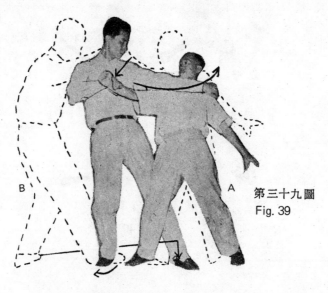

第三十九圖
Fig. 39

第四法——截蹬腿

此法乃係以腿破腿法之一。乘敵以「挑腿」，或「鴛鴦腿」等法攻我時，可施此法破之。

圖解：設我與敵爭鬥間，見敵以「挑腿」法向我下陰挑來，即乘其腿將及未到之際，身向側閃，同時舉右腿反挑其腿彎。見第四十圖。

承上式，我用挑腿截住其挑腿，即配合身向左後閃仰之勢，勁貫脚跟橫蹬敵之下陰，則敵死矣。見第四十一圖。

按：敵腿勁被截，勢必失，是時乘隙反攻，創敵必矣。

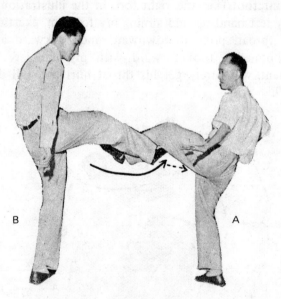

第四十圖
Fig. 40

TECHNIQUE 4 — INTERSECTING KICK

This technique is one of those which use legs to repel foot strokes. When the opponent are using such techniques as "Picking Kick" or "Couple Kicks" to attack me, I can use this technique to defeat him.

ILLUSTRATIONS: Supposing I am fighting with the opponent and I see him picking his foot up against my private part with the technique of Picking Kick, before his foot reaches me, dodging to one side, I lift my right leg to pick the foot up against the hollow of his knee. See Fig. 40.

Following the preceding movement, I use my foot to intercept his leg, and then dodging and leaning to the left backside, I transfer my strength onto my heel and strike transversely at his private part. If it hits the mark, the opponent will be killed. See Fig. 41.

When the opponent's leg is intersected, he will surely lose his offensive. At that moment, if I take advantage of his blunder and counter-attack him, I can surely injure him.

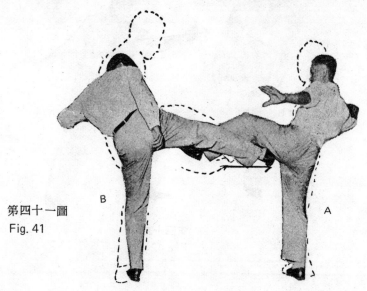

第四十一圖
Fig. 41

B

A

第五法——彈腿

此法乃係乘敵一拳擊來，或抓來之時，我閃之而反傷其上下五寸部位之法。

圖解：設我行立間，突見敵上步，欲以右手抓我右肩，企圖施「摔角術」摔我，或其他手法謀我。我即乘其右手將抓住而未逞時，略提左脚，配合身向左傾側之勢，左脚落地，同時施斜彈勁，將右脚彈出；照準敵前步上下五寸處，以足外緣施彈勁彈擊之。見第四十二圖。

按：此腿一中，則敵必捧腿而歸。蓋上下五寸處（即迎面骨），肉少而神經多，輕擊之其痛無比，雖壯漢亦不可忍也。

第四十二圖
Fig. 42

TECHNIQUE 5 — SNAPPING KICK

This technique is to dodge an opponent's blow with his fist or his seizure and counter-hurt his tibia.

ILLUSTRATIONS: Supposing when I am standing or walking, I see the opponent moving toward me, going to seize me on my right shoulder with his right hand and attempting to trip me up with the technique of wrestling, or using other means to attack me, before his right hand reaches my shoulder, I lift my left foot a little, and inclining my body to the left, drop my left foot on the ground; at the same time, I snap my right foot out, exerting a slanting elastic force; aiming at the tibia of the opponent's front foot, strike at it, exerting an elastic force, with the lateral side of my right foot. See Fig. 42.

If the foot hits the mark, the opponent will certainly retreat by holding his leg because a tibia is not fleshy but many-nerved, which will feel intolerably painful even when lightly hit. Even a strong man cannot bear the pain.

第六法——割腿

此法乃係乘敵欲上步謀我時，我突施此法割其前步而創之之法。

圖解：設我見敵欲上左步出拳擊我之時，即乘其左步剛一踏實之際，身向後側，同時以右腳外緣，施割訣由左向右如以鋸鋸木然，照準敵左小腿上下五寸之處施斜勁割之。見第四十三圖。

承上式，敵腿被割，必苦痛難忍，而致心散意失，影響其步向後縮，而身向前傾。是時我即乘其上身向前傾之勢，右手以手背拳端，配合身向右前翻之勢，施勁向敵面部擊下。見第四十四圖。

按：此法一應，敵下則腿步被截，上則眼面被封，大勢已失，無可反抗，受制必矣。

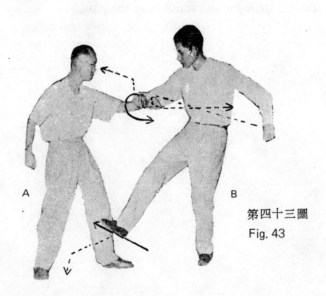

第四十三圖
Fig. 43

TECHNQUE 6 – CUTTING KICK

This technique is to cut an opponent's front foot suddenly and hurt it when he is moving forward to attack me.

ILLUSTRATIONS: Supposing I see the opponent moving his left foot forward to attack me with his fist, as soon as he sets his left foot on the ground, leaning my body backward, I snap my right foot from left to right and cut his left shin, exerting a slanting force, with the lateral side of the foot as if cutting a log with a saw. See Fig. 43.

Following the preceding movement, as his leg is cut, he will surely feel too painful to bear, he will surely be distracted, which causes him to draw his foot back and lean his body forward; when he leans his body forward, strike forcefully at his face with the back end of my right fist, turning my body right to the front. See Fig. 44.

If this technique is used, I shall certainly defeat the opponent because he cannot resist any longer and can do nothing about it when his foot is cut and his eyes and face are attacked.

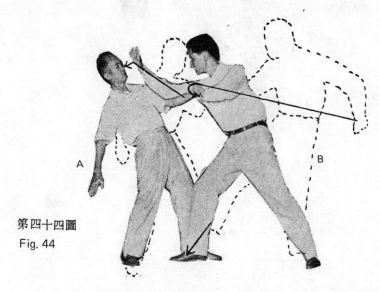

第四十四圖
Fig. 44

71

第七法──橫蹬腿

此法乃係乘敵一拳擊來，我巧蹬敵脇部，斷其肋骨而創之之法。

圖解：設我與敵交手之間，見敵上右步，右拳照我胸部擊來。我即乘其來拳將及未到之際，身向右後轉，同時右拳撥格其腕或肘部。見第四十五圖。

承上式，我配合左手由下穿上撥格其腕部之勢，坐腰沉氣，重心移於右步，施蹬訣直勁，以左足後跟向敵右腋下脇肋部蹬去。見第四十六圖。

按：此腿如能適迎敵向我衝來之勢，則敵肋骨必折一二條。

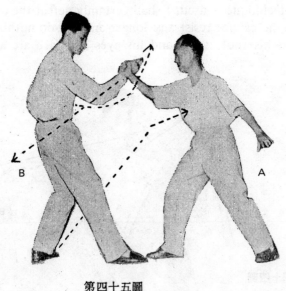

第四十五圖
Fig. 45

TECHNIQUE 7 — TRANSVERSE KICK

This technique is to strike skilfully at an opponent's costal region and hurt him by breaking his ribs when he is attacking me with his fist.

ILLUSTRATIONS: Supposing when I am fighing with the opponent, I see him moving his right foot forward and giving me a blow at my chest with his right fist, before his fist reaches my chest, I turn my body right to the back, holding his wrist or elbow back with my right fist. See Fig. 45.
Following the preceding movement, threading my left hand up from below to poke his wrist, lower my waist and sink my strength to shift the centre of gravity onto the right foot; then exerting a straight force in the trick of Straight-kicking, I snap my left heel against his costal region under the right armpit. See Fig. 46.
If the foot can meet his attack against me, it will surely break one or two of his ribs.

第四十六圖
Fig. 46

第八法——膝撩腿

此法乃係當我與敵交手間，欲重創之，突施而巧取其命之法。

圖解：設我與敵交手之際，而欲出重招傷敵時，先以右手中食二指向前探取敵之雙眼（此爲虛着），敵見我迎取其雙眼，必然身向後仰，而避我勢。見第四十七圖。

承上式，乘敵身向後仰，其手欲格我右手之勢，我即將右手縮回，同時順勢施腰勁身向後抽仰，乘勢提右膝，施撞訣上彈勁。以膝頭照準敵之下陰撞去（此爲實着）。見第四十八圖。

按：此腿如着敵，不死亦重創。如非迫不得已，可撞敵小腹部位，制之可矣，不必定取其命也。

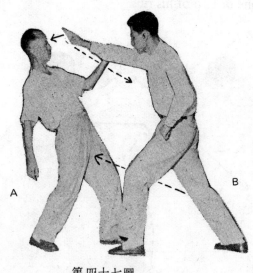

第四十七圖
Fig. 47

TECHNIQUE 8 — KNEE-SCOOPING KICK

This technique is to be abruptly used to kill an opponent if I want to hurt him heavily when I am fighting with him.

ILLUSTRATIONS: Supposing I am going to hurt the opponent with a heavy blow when I am fighting with him, I reach my right index and middle fingers forward for his eyes (this is a false movement); when he find me attacking his eyes, he will surely lean backward to dodge my attack. See Fig. 47. Following the preceding movement, when he is leaning his body backward and going to hold my right hand back with his hand, draw my right hand back; at the same time, drawing my body backward accordingly with the force of my waist, lift my right knee, and exerting an elastic force in the trick of Bumping, bump into his private part (this is a real movement) with the knee. See Fig. 48.

If the knee hits the mark, the opponent will be seriously hurt even if he is not killed; unless I have no alternative, I can only defeat him by bumping into his lower abdomen and it is not necessary to kill him.

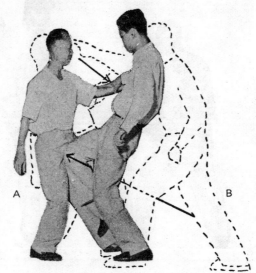

第四十八圖
Fig. 48

75

第九法——彈蹬腿

此法乃係敗中取勝之法。當我踢出之腿被敵擒住時，可施此法反創之。

圖解：設我與敵交手之際，見敵有隙可乘，即上步起右腿挑敵下陰。不料敵虛中有實，一不留神，右腿反被敵擒住。見第四十九圖。

承上式，我右腿一被敵擒住，是時必需鎮靜，乘敵未施其他手法謀我之前，身立即向下坐，配合施腰勁身向左後轉之勢，突施蹬訣彈直勁，以右足後跟（足尖向下翻），照準敵之心窩反蹬。見第五十圖。

按：此腿如蹬着，敵不但即放擒我腿之雙手，且必重創倒地；蓋我轉身反撐之勁力極猛，且心窩爲要害也。

第四十九圖
Fig. 49

TECHNIQUE 9 — BACK-SNAPPING KICK

This is a technique for winning in adverse conditions; it is used to counter-hurt an opponent when he is seizing my going foot.

ILLUSTRATIONS: Supposing I find there is an opportunity to take advantage of when I am fighting with the opponent, I move forward, lift my right foot and pick it up against his private part; but unexpectedly as his false movement contains a real intention, my foot is, on the contrary, caught by him due to my carelessness for the time being. See Fig. 49. Following the preceding movement, as soon as my right foot is caught by him, I must keep calm, and before he uses other means to attack me, I lower my body, and turning my body left to the back with the force of the waist, snap my right heel (with the tip of the foot turned downward) with a straight force in the trick of Straight-kicking against his cavity of stomach. See Fig. 50.
If the foot hits the mark, the opponent will not only loosen his two hands catching my foot, but fall on the ground due to serious in-
jury because the back-snap-ping force is very violent and the cavity of stomach is a vital part.

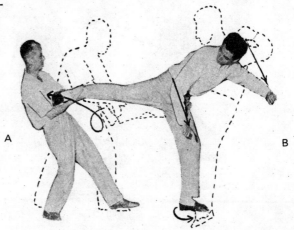

第五十圖
Fig. 50

77

第十法——鈎絆腿

此法乃係乘敵一拳擊來時，我封其來手，而反跌之之法。

　　圖解：設我與敵爭論之間，見敵突上右步，右拳當胸擊來。如我不欲傷之，即乘其來拳將及未到之際，用左手由外在敵右肘內彎處，向下向左圈纏，使敵右臂一時被困而向外傾。見第五十一圖。

　　承上式，我一面纏困敵之右臂，同時上右步置敵右步之後方，配合我右掌往左上方推其心窩或喉部之勁，左腿施鈎絆訣斜勁，以足後脛向後鈎絆其右步，則敵重心一傾，必往左後方仰跌。見第五十二圖。

　　按：敵來拳為直勁，我以橫圈勁中途截之，則敵直力被破而中停，一時不能換勁，故受困。

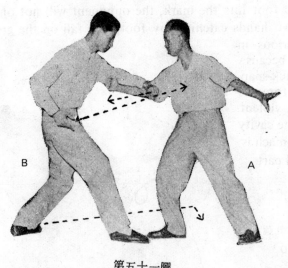

第五十一圖

Fig. 51

TECHNIQUE 10 – HOOKING AND TRIPPING

This technique is to block an opponent's coming hand when he is giving me a blow with one fist and trip him up.

ILLUSTRATIONS: Supposing I see the opponent moving his right foot forward and striking at my chest with his right fist when I am arguing with him, if I don't want to injure him, before his fist reaches my chest, I circle my left hand down from outside and put it round his right elbow so as to press his right arm outward to the left for the time being. See Fig. 51.

Following the preceding movement, when I am pressing his right arm outward, I move my right foot forward to the back side of his right foot; pushing my right palm upward to the left against his cavity of stomach or his throat, I hook and trip his right foot with the back of my left shin backward, exerting a slanting force in the trick of Hooking and Tripping. Then his centre of gravity is shifted to one side and he will surely fall supine to the left backside. See Fig. 52.

As the opponent uses a straight force in throwing his fist against me, the force will be broken off and cannot be changed for the time being if I intersect his arm midway with a circling force, so the opponent will be cornered.

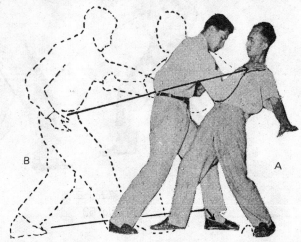

第五十二圖

Fig. 52

79

第十一法——穿心腿

此法乃係乘敵欲封我手部反攻時，我突出穿心腿，反傷其心窩之法。

圖解：設我與敵交手間，我見有隙可乘，即上左步，以右拳擊敵之胸部（此爲虛着）。敵見我右拳擊來，必以左掌向上向外撥格，企圖反攻。見第五十三圖。

承上式，敵一用左掌穿格我右臂，即空其勢，乘其全神注意右臂之際，我身向後仰，施腰勁順勢以蹬訣，出右腿足踵閃斜向上，足尖回反，使足心向上，向前上方對準敵之心窩蹬去。見第五十四圖。

按：穿心腿乃少林寺正宗最難學習，最難施用，亦最難預防之腿法。

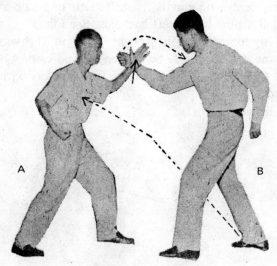

第五十三圖
Fig. 53

TECHNIQUE 11 — HEART-HITTING KICK

This technique is to make a sudden heart-hittin gkick to counter-hurt an opponent's cavity of stomach when he is going to block my hand for a counter-attack.

ILLUSTRATIONS: Supposing I find an opportunity to take advantage of when I am fighting with the opponent, I move my left foot forward and strike at his chest with my right fist (this is a false movement); when he sees my right fist coming, he will surely poke it upward and outward with his left palm, attempting to counter-attack. See Fig. 53. Following the preceding movement, as soon as he uses his left palm to hold back my right arm, I withdraw my offensive secretly, when he is paying attention to my right arm, leaning my body backward, I snap my right heel up slantingly with the tip of the foot pointing back to face the sole upward, exerting the force of the waist accordingly and aiming the foot up forward at the opponent's cavity of stomach, and strike at it. See Fig. 54.

As the Heart-hitting Kick is the orthodox technique of the haolin School, it is the most difficult to learn, the most difficult to use and the most difficult to prevent.

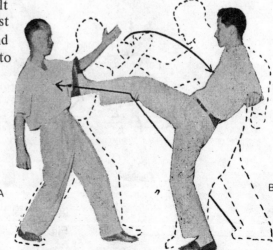

第五十四圖
Fig. 54

A

B

81

第十二法——偷踹腿

此法乃係乘敵起腿踢我時，我反起腿傷之之法。屬以腿破腿法之一。

圖解：設我與敵交手間，見敵突然上步施右挑腿法，企圖挑撩我下陰部。我即乘其來腿將及之際，身略向左轉，順勢將右腿向上彎提，格開敵之右足。見第五十五圖。

承上式，我一格開敵之右足，即施蹬訣彈勁，配合身向左後緩轉之勢，照準敵之左後步膝側處，用右斜蹬。見第五十六圖。

按：敵膝側被蹬，即不脫臼亦必跌地，因其支持重心之後步被橫取故也。

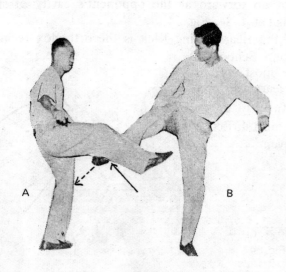

第五十五圖
Fig. 55

TECHNIQUE 12 – SNEAK KICK

This technique is to counter-hurt an opponent with a foot when he is striking at me with his foot. It falls under the techniques which use feet to repel foot strokes.

ILLUSTRATIONS: Supposing I see the opponent suddenly moving forward and picking his right foot up against my private part when I am fighting with him, before his foot reaches me, turning my body slightly to the left, bend and lift my right leg up accordingly to hold his right foot back. See Fig. 55.

Following the preceding movement, after I have held his right foot back, turning my body slowly left to the back, I aim my right foot at the knee of his rear leg (i.e. the left one in the illustration) and strike slantingly at it, exerting an elastic force in the trick of Straight-kicking. See Fig. 56.

If the side of the opponent's knee is hit, he will surely fall on the ground even though his knee is not dislocated, because his rear foot supporting his body weight is transversely attacked.

第五十六圖

Fig. 56   A   B

83

第十三法——圈彈腿

此法乃乘敵起腿踢我時，我反以腿法取其命之法。屬以腿破腿法之一。

圖解：設我與敵交手之際，見敵突飛起右腿，欲踹我左前腿上下五寸處。我即乘其來腿將及之際，略退左步，閃開其勢，同時重心穩定，順勢用右腿以足背挑擊敵踢來之膝內彎，打散敵右腿之直勁。見第五十七圖。

承上式，我一將敵之來勁擊散，即配合身向左後轉之勢，右腿向左方轉圈形，以彈訣用足踵由下向上，施彈勁彈擊敵之下陰。見第五十八圖。

按：此圈彈之法，一挑一彈必須貫於一氣，不可中斷。

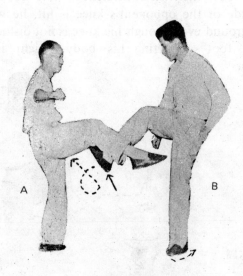

第五十七圖
Fig. 57

84

TECHNIQUE 13 – CIRCLING AND SNAPPING

This is a technique to kill an opponent with foot strokes when he is striking at me with his foot. It is also one of the techniques which use legs to repel foot strokes.

ILLUSTRATIONS: Supposing I see the opponent suddenly flying his right foot at the tibia of my left front leg when I am fighting with him, before his foot reaches my leg, drawing my left foot back to dodge his offensive and keeping my centre of gravity steady, I pick my right foot up accordingly against the hollow of his right knee with the back of the foot so as to break up the straight force of his right foot. See Fig. 57.
Following the preceding movement, as soon as I break up his coming force, turning my body left to the back, I circle my right foot to the left and snap its heel up from below against his private part, exerting an elastic force. See Fig. 58.
In this technique of Circling and Snapping, the picking and snapping must be done at a stretch without any intervals.

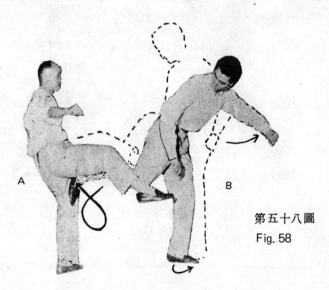

第五十八圖
Fig. 58

第十四法——探喉腿

此法乃係乘敵以腿或拳，取我中盤時，我反創之之法。

圖解：設我與敵交手間，敵突然施用穿心拳法，取我心窩要害。我即乘其拳尚未到之際，急出左手，攔截其右腕，同時重心穩於左前步，以待變式。見第五十九圖。

承上式，我重心一穩定，即配合上身向右後仰之勢，貫勁於右足外緣，由下向上向外，對準敵之喉部割去。見第六十圖。

按：此法極巧，不但因身之仰後而避開敵之穿心拳，同時順勢反割傷其喉部。

第五十九圖

Fig. 59

86

TECHNIQUE 14 — THROAT-REACHING KICK

This technique is to counter-hurt an opponent when he is striking at my medium part with his foot or fist.

ILLUSTRATION: Supposing the opponent is suddenly striking at the vital part of my cavity of stomach with a technique of heart-hitting boxing when I am fighting with him, before his fist hits the mark, I quickly rush my left hand out to intersept his right wrist; at the same time, keeping my centre of gravity steady on my left front foot, wait for the change of styles. See Fig. 59.

Following the preceding movement, as soon as I get my centre of gravity steady, leaning my body to the right back-side, I transfer my strength onto the lateral side of the right foot and cut his throat upward and outward from below with it. See Fig. 60.

This technique is very clever because it enables me not only to dodge the opponent's heart-hitting fist by means of leaning back, but to injure his throat accordingly with the trick of cutting.

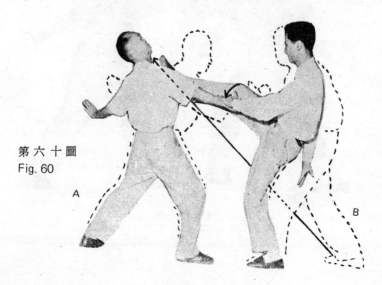

第六十圖
Fig. 60

A

B

第十五法——撞心腿

此法乃係乘敵一拳擊來時，我封其來手，而反以膝磕傷其心窩之法。

圖解：設我與敵交手間，見敵上右步，以右手當胸擊來。我即乘其來拳將及未到之間，身略向左閃，重心移於左步，同時出右手，由下抄上將敵之右腕抓住。見第六十一圖。

承上式，我右手一將敵之右腕抓住，同時左手抄上攄住其右肘部，施勁向我右後方拉挫；同時配合雙手之拉勁，施撞訣斜勁，勁貫右膝頭，對準敵之心窩撞去，敵必大創。見第六十二圖。

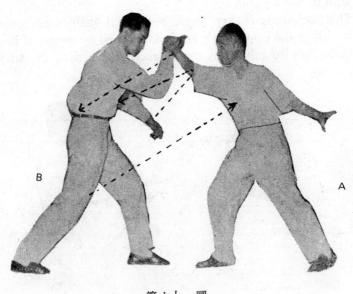

第六十一圖
Fi. 61

TECHNIQUE 15 — HEART-KNOCKING KICK

This technique is to block an opponent's attacking fist and counter-hurt his cavity of stomach with a knee when he is giving me a blow.

ILLUSTRATIONS: Supposing the opponent is moving his right foot forward and striking at my chest with his right hand when I am fighting with him, before his fist reaches me, dodging slightly to the left and shifting the centre of gravity onto my left foot, I rush my right hand out, scoop it up from below and seize his right wrist. See Fig. 61.

Following the preceding movement, as soon as I seize the opponent's right wrist with my right hand, scooping my left hand up to catch his right elbow, I draw and press it forcefully to my right backside; at the same time when I am drawing his right arm with my hands, I transfer my strength onto my right knee and knock at his cavity of stomach, exerting a slanting force in the trick of Bumping. Then the opponent will surely be seriously hurt. See Fig. 62.

第六十二圖
Fig. 62

89

第十六法——跺膝腿

此法乃係乘敵以掃蹚腿掃我時，我以跺訣反斷其腿之法。屬以腿破腿法之一。

圖解： 設我與敵交手之際，見敵中上部有隙，即上左步，用左拳照敵面部擊去。孰料敵虛中有實，見我照其頭部打去，突移重心於左步，身向下縮，同時施掃訣橫勁，用右腿由右向左，以掃蹚腿法掃我左腿脛。見第六十三圖。

承上式，我見敵突以右腿掃來，即乘其腿尚未到時，急身向左轉，穩定重心左手；同時施跺訣下勁，以勁貫於右足，配合身向下坐之勢，以右足迎勁照準敵之右膝磕跺下。見第六十四圖。

按：此腿跺着，則不但可破其勢，且其膝節必脫臼無疑矣。

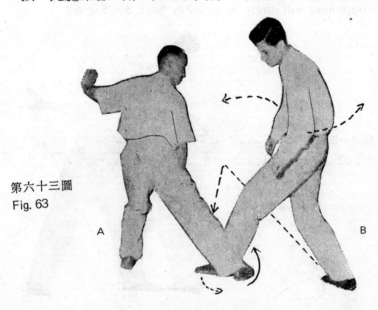

第六十三圖
Fig. 63

A   B

TECHNIQUE 16 – KNEE-STAMPING KICK

This technique is to counter-break an opponent's leg with the trick of Stamping when he is sweeping me with his foot. It is one of the techniques which use feet to repel foot strokes.

ILLUSTRATIONS: Supposing I see a loophole at the opponent's upper and medium parts when I am fighting with him, I move my left foot forward and rush my left fist against his face, but I don't expect that he has concealed a real intention in his false movement, so when he sees me striking at his head, he suddenly shifts his centre of gravity onto his right foot and lower his body; at the same time, exerting a transverse force in the trick of Sweeping, he sweeps my left shin with his right foot from right to left. See Fig. 63.

Following the preceding movement, when I see the opponent sweeping me suddenly with his right foot, before his foot reaches me, I turn my body quickly to the left, keeping my centre of gravity steady on the left foot; at the same time, exerting a downward force in the trick of Stamping, I transfer my strength onto the right foot, and lowering my body, I stamp my right foot onto his right knee against his attacking force. See Fig. 64.

If my foot hits the mark, I shall not only repel his offensive, but also dislocate his knee joint without doubt.

第六十四圖
Fig. 64

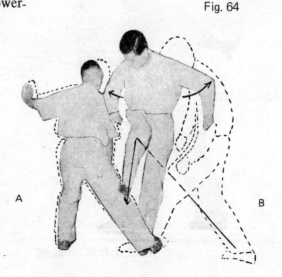

A

B

91

第十七法——立鴛鴦腿

此法乃係乘敵從後打我時，我反身施連環腿擊，而反取其命之法。屬敗中取勝腿法之一。

圖解：設我與敵交手間，見敵架工勢勇，一時難以取勝時，即反身做敗走之狀。敵見吾敗走，勢必趕步追擊；是時即乘其來拳將及之際，突收步將重心移於右步，向身下沉，趁勢起左腿施蹬訣彈勁，反身向敵之胸腹蹬去。見第六十五圖。

承上式，我突起左腿反蹬敵，如果敵身敏步捷，能急中後退。是時我見腿不中敵，即急將左步放下穩固重心，身向左後轉，同時配合身之轉勢，施挑訣上勁，用右足背照準敵之下陰由下向上挑擊。見第六十六圖。

按：此腿不施則已，施之敵必難逃。蓋敵雖身手敏捷，在瞬息之間，難防連環兩腿也。

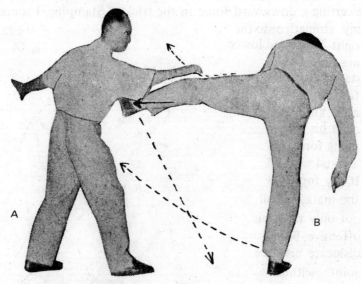

第六十五圖　Fig. 65

TECHNIQUE 17 — STANDING COUPLE KICKS

This technique is to turn the body back and strike with both feet in a running way to kill an opponent when he is giving me a blow from behind. It is one of the foot striking techniques for winning in an adverse state.

ILLUSTRATIONS: Supposing I find that the opponent's force of fending off is so powerful that I am unable to defeat him for the time being when I am fighting with him, I pretend to lose the field and take to flight by turning my body back; when the opponent finds me taking to flight, he will certainly follow up; at that time when his fist is approaching me, stopping my movement suddenly, shifting my centre of gravity onto my right foot and sinking my body, I lift my left foot up accordingly and snap it against his chest and abdomen by turning my body back, exerting a snapping force in the trick of Straight-kicking. See Fig. 65.

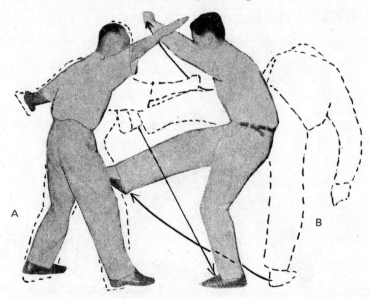

第六十六圖　Fig. 66

第十八法──臥鴛奮腿

此法乃係當我跌倒，或故意跌倒，乘敵欲上前謀我時，突施連環腿而創敵之法。屬敗中取勝腿法之一。

圖解：設我與敵交手之間，見敵勢勇架工，一時甚難取勝，即假做敗走，繼而滑跌，跌時以右小臂及腕着地襯勢，以備反攻。是時敵見我敗中滑跌，不論眞僞，勢必趨前企圖傷我。我即乘敵乘勢進擊之際，將在上之左足，施蹬訣直勁，蹬敵之脅部，以阻敵之進攻。見第六十七圖。

承上式，我以左足蹬敵之左步，不論蹬中與否，右掌施勁向地一捺，上身向左仰，使背部完全離地。同時配合左掌捺地之勢，施腰勁上身突然躍起，收回左腳，即施蹬訣彈勁，用右足踵照敵之心窩要害蹬去。見第六十八圖。

按：此時敵或連中二腿，或僅中一腿，亦必負創倒地，我可乘機右足落翻勁起身，繼而制之矣。

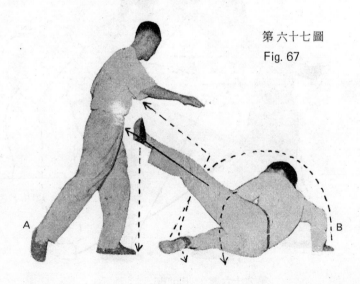

第 六 十 七 圖
Fig. 67

94

Following the preceding movement. When I snap my foot up suddenly to counter-attack the opponent, if the opponent is quick in motion, he can retreat in haste; at that time, when my foot does not hit the mark, I shall drop my foot abruptly on the ground to keep my centre of gravity steady and turn my body left to the back; at the same time when I am turning my body, exerting an upward force in the trick of Picking, pick my right foot up from below and strike at his private part with the back of the foot. See Fig. 66.

Nothing will happen if these kicks are not used, but the opponent will surely be unable to escape if they are used because he is difficult guard against the running snapping of both feet in the twinkling of an eye although he is quick in motion.

TECHNIQUE 18 — LYING COUPLE KICKS

This technique is to snap both feet out in a running way to injure an opponent when I fall down or deliberately fall down at the moment the opponent move forward to attack me. This is one of the foot striking techniques for winning in an adverse state.

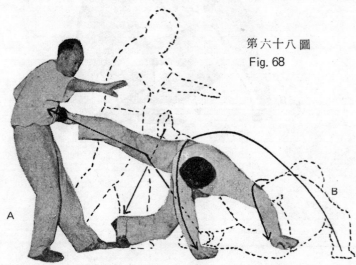

第六十八 圖
Fig. 68

第十九法——鈎蹬腿

此法乃係乘敵一拳擊來時，閃而斷其腿之法。

圖解：設我與敵交手之際，見敵突然一拳迎面擊來，欲閃不及，急以左手護頭，右手反上抓敵之右腕（抓不住亦可）。同時施腰勁，側身左後閃跌（跌時以左小臂及肘先着地），以左足背順跌勢將敵之右脚脛用勁鈎住，向我方鈎拉，並同時以右足心，配合左脚背之鈎勁，施冷勁照敵之右膝上約二三寸處，向外一蹬，則敵之右腿必斷。見第六十九圖。

第六十九圖
Fig. 69

ILLUSTRATIONS: Supposing I find that the opponent's force of fending off is so powerful that I am uneasy to win for the time being when I am fighting with him, I pretend to lose the field and take to flight, then I slip and fall, supporting myself wth my right forearm and wrist on the ground for the purpose to counter-attack; at that time as the opponent sees me slip and fall, disregarding whether it is true or false, he will surely move forward in an attempt to injure me; when he is going to attack, I snap the hanging left foot against his costal region, exerting a straight force in the trick of Straight-kicking, so as to check him from attacking me. See Fig. 67.

Following the preceding movement, no matter whether my left foot hits the mark or not, I press my right palm forcefully down against the ground, inclining my upper body to the left to lift my back completely away from the ground; pressing my left palm down on the ground and exerting the force of my waist, I jerk my upper body suddenly up, draw my left foot back and snap my right heel against the opponent's vital part in his cavity of stomach, exerting a snapping force in the trick of Straight-kicking. See Fig. 68.

At this time, no matter whether one or both of the opponent's legs are hit, he will surely be hurt and fall on the ground. Then I can take advantage of the opportunity, turn and drop my right foot down on the ground and spring up to my feet, further defeating him.

TECHNQIUE 19 — HOOKING AND KICKING

This technique is to dodge an opponent's blow with his fist and break one of his legs.

ILLUSTRATIONS: Supposing I see the opponent suddenly striking at my face with his fist when I am fighting with him and it is too late for me to dodge, quickly protecting my head with my left hand, I turn my right hand up and

第二十法——絞腿

此法乃係乘敵一拳擊來，我閃避不及時，反跌敵之法。屬敗中取勝之法。

圖解：設我與敵交手之際，敵突然止步一拳當胸擊來，勢急而不及閃避，即施腰勁，身向後翻左側跌下，以左肘左肩着地支持重心，同時配合身向後翻仰之勢，左腿向敵步前伸，右腿向敵步後伸，以迎力將敵胯部挾緊。見第七十圖。

承上式，我兩腿一將敵之腿部挾緊，即施腰勁身向右挺轉，用鈎絆訣斜橫勁，左腿向敵後方鈎，右腿向敵前方絆壓，形成迎力絞式。是時敵必因我之鈎絆，而失却重心，向前仆跌。見第七十一圖。

第七十圖
Fig. 70

98

seize his right wrist (it doesn't matter to miss it); at the same time, exerting the force of my waist, I incline my body to the left backside and fall on the ground (when falling, drop the left forearm and elbow on the ground first); in the course of falling, I hook the opponent's right shin forcefully with the back of my left foot and pull it to my side; at the same time, in coordination with the hooking of the left foot, snap my right sole suddenly outward at one or two inches above his right knee. Then his right leg will surely be broken. See Fig. 69.

TECHNIQUE 20 — LEG TWISTING

This technique is to counter-fell an opponent when it is too late for me to dodge his blow with his fist. It is a technique to win in an adverse state.

ILLUSTRATIONS: Supposing the opponent stops moving forward, rushing a fist against my chest, when I am fighting with him and it is too late for me to dodge owing to the swiftness of his attack, exerting the force of my waist at

第七十一圖
Fig. 71

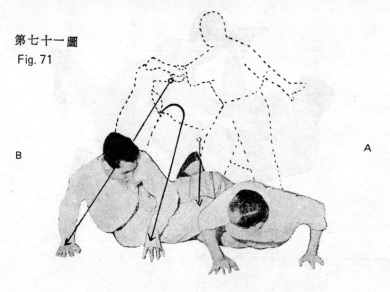

B

A

第二十一法——挾剪腿

此法乃係乘敵一拳擊來，我突閃而挾其腰部，剪其內部取其命之法。屬敗中取勝之法。

圖解：設我與敵交手之際，敵突然上步當胸一拳擊來，我不及還手，急以右手抓住敵之左腕（抓不住亦可），同時用腰勁一挺，身向後翻仰，以雙肘或單肘支持着地，雙腿往上往前衝，如老樹盤根式，迎面將敵肋骨以下之軟腰挾住，雙脚互相鈎掛，施挾剪訣橫勁，迎合雙脛互相鈎別之勁，用雙膝往裏迎力挾剪敵人之腰部，並往下墜使敵跪地，（此時可乘機以背臀着地，雙手防敵之雙手），待喊痛求饒為止。見第七十二圖。

按：如敵尚欲頑強反抗，只要雙腿施力猛挾，則不難使敵之橫隔膜破裂而亡。

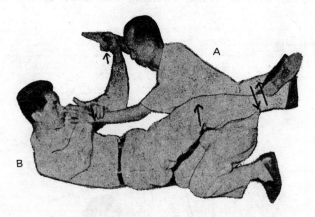

第七十二圖

Fig. 72

once, I turn my body back and fall on the left side, supporting my bodyweight with the left elbow and shoulder; at the same time, in coordination with the turning and inclining of my body, I stretch my left foot to front of his leg and my right foot to the back of the leg and clamp the opponent's leg tightly with opposite forces. See Fig. 70.

Following the preceding movement, as soon as my two legs clamp the opponent's leg tightly, exerting the force of my waist, I lift and turn my body to the right; with slanting and transverse forces in the tricks of Hooking and Tripping, hook my left leg to the back of the opponent and press my right leg to his front, thus twisting his leg with the opposite forces of my legs. At that time, the opponent will surely lose his centre of gravity and fall prostrate to the front due to my hooking and tripping. See Fig. 71.

TECHNIQUE 21 — CLAMPING AND CLIPPING

This technique is to dodge an opponent's blow with his fist suddenly, clamp his waist and clip his internal organs to kill him. It is one of the technique to win in an adverse state.

ILLUSTRATIONS: Supposing the opponent suddenly moves forward and rushes his fist against my chest when I am fighting with him and it is too late for me to counter-attack, I quickly seize his left wrist with my right hand (it doesn't matter to miss it); at the same time, I throw my waist up forcefully and incline my body backward, supporting it with both or one of my elbows on the ground; rush both legs up forward and clamp the opponent's soft loins below his ribs like roots winding an old tree, both feet hooking each other and exerting a transverse force in the tricks of Clamping and Clipping; in coordination with the mutual hooking of both shins, I clamp and clip his waist with both knees exerting inward opposite forces to make him fall and squat on the ground (at this time, I can take advantages of the opportunity to fall with my back and hip on the ground and use my hands to guard against his hands) until he begs for mercy due to

第二十二法——單飛腿

此法乃係乘敵起拳來擊時，我以腿封之而反傷其面喉等部之法。

圖解：設我與敵爭論之間，敵突上右步以右拳擊我，即乘其來拳將及之際，身向後仰，順勢起左腿（虛招）以挑訣挑擊敵之右肘部。見第七十三圖。

承上式，敵見我左腿挑去（虛招），定必身向後仰或後退，同時右手下抄擒我左腿。是時即急乘其身略向前傾，用手擒我右腿之勢，急提氣躍起，配合左腿回縮之勁，右腿施點訣彈勁，對準敵之喉部點蹴，敵必重創。見第七十四圖。

第七十三圖
Fig. 73

pains. See Fig. 72.

If the opponent continues to resist stubbornly, it is not difficult to kill him by breaking his diaphragm so long as I clamp his waist forcefully with my legs.

TECHNIQUE 22 — SINGLE FLYING KICK

This technique is to fend off an opponent's blow with my foot and counter-hurt his face or throad.

ILLUSTRATIONS: Supposing the opponent suddenly moves his right foot forward and rushes his right fist against me when I am disputing with him before his fist reaches me, leaning my body back, I lift my left foot accordingly (a false move) and strike at his right elbow with the trick of Picking. See Fig. 73.

Following the preceding movement, when the opponent sees my left foot going against him (a false move), he will surely lean his body back or retreat, moving his right hand down to catch my left foot; at this time when he is leaning his body slightly forward to seize my left foot, I quickly spring up

第七十四圖

Fig. 74

A

B

103

第二十三法——雙飛腿

此法乃係我與敵交手間，乘敵轉身之際，突施之而傷敵之法。

圖解：設我與敵交手間，乘敵轉身換式之際，突施腰勁，氣向上提，身向上蹤，先四肢內含，如抱球狀。見第七十五圖。

承上式，全身凌空，配合雙手施勁外分之勢，雙足施蹬訣彈勁，對準敵人背部「對心穴」蹬去，敵必重創。見第七十六圖。

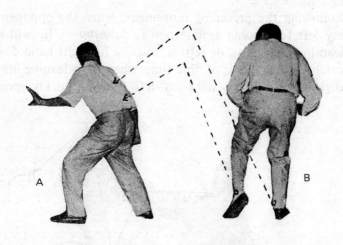

第七十五圖
Fig. 75

104

by heaving my strength; drawing my left foot back, I snap
my right foot at his throat with a snapping force in the trick
of Shoving. Then the opponent will surely be seriously hurt.
See Fig. 74.

TECHNIQUE 23 – DOUBLE FLYING KICK

This technique is to be abruptly used to injure an opponent
when he is turning round in the fight.

ILLUSTRATION: Supposing the opponentis turning round to
change his posture when I am fighting with him, suddenly
exerting the force of my waist, heaving my strength and
springing up, move four limbs inward as if holding a ball
in the arms. See Fig. 75.
Following the preceding movement, staying in the air and
parting both hands outward forcefully, snap both feet at
the heart location of the opponent's back with a snapping
force in the trick of Straight-kicking. Then the opponent will
surely be seriously hurt. See Fig. 76.

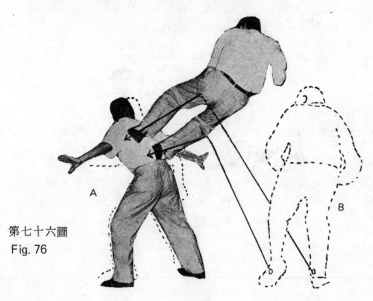

第七十六圖
Fig. 76

第二十四法——滾剪腿

此腿乃係乘敵上右步擊我時，我閃而剪折其腿部之法。

圖解：設我與敵交手間，見敵上右步，欲出拳擊我，即乘其拳將出之際，身向右偏閃，雙手着地支持體重，順勢右腿在下，向敵右步前伸插，左腿向上，向敵右步後伸至腿彎部位。見第七十七圖。

承上式，俟我一將敵之右步別住，即施腰勁身向右後轉滾，同時配合腰勁右轉滾之勢，兩腿施小腿勁絞別敵之右腿（左脛別敵右腿彎，右後脛別敵右前脛）則敵必仆跌。見第七十八圖。

第七十七圖
Fig. 77

TECHNIQUE 24 — ROLLING AND CLIPPING

This technique is to dodge and clip to break an opponent's leg when he is moving his right foot forward to attack me.

ILLUSTRATIONS: Supposing the opponent is moving his right foot forward in an attempt to give me a blow with his fist when I am fighting with him, before his fist is goint out, I dodget and incline to the right with both hands touching the ground to support my bodyweight; accordingly, I stretch my right leg which is lower to front of his right foot; I stretch my left leg which is higher up to the hollow of his right knee. See Fig. 77.

Following the preceding movement, as soon as I clamp his right leg, I roll my body with the force of my waist to the right backside, at the same time, in coordination with the rolling, I clip and twist his right leg with both legs, exerting the force of the shanks (the left shin used to clip the hollow of his right knee and the back of the right shin used to clip the front of his right shin). Then the opponent will surely be tripped up. See Fig. 78.

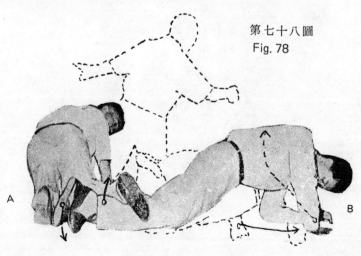

第七十八圖
Fig. 78

承上式，一將敵之右步絞緊，身向右後繼續翻滾，順勢配合左脛向左脛鉤別敵之右腿彎之勁，施腰勁以右後脛向右向下別壓敵之前脛，則敵必被困而不能動彈。見第七十九圖。

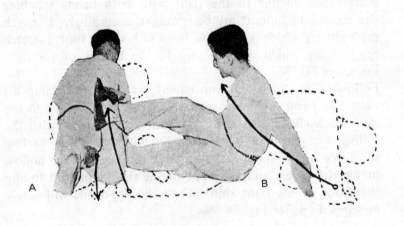

第七十九圖
Fig. 79

Following the preceding movement, as soon as I twist his right foot tightly, I continue to roll my body to the right backside, and accordingly, hooking the hollow of his right knee to the left with my left shin, I clip and press the front of his right shin down to the right with the back of my right shin, exerting the force of my waist; then the opponent will surely be too tightly twisted to move. See Fig. 79.

附錄：練腿基本功

一、壓　腿

甲　正壓——按腿

動作：1. 面對訓練工具（桌、凳、墻、窗台或肋木，以後說到的工具，皆指這些而言），離開兩小步站立。

2. 將右脚跟擱在工具上，高度與小腹相平，脚尖上翹，膝部挺直；左脚支持身體，脚尖對訓練工具，膝部挺直。

3. 雙手五指交叉，按在右膝上；目視右脚尖。

4. 兩肘彎曲，上身前俯，然後還原，接着再前俯（圖一）。右腿經過數次俯壓之後，放下，換左腿擱上。

目的：訓練股二頭肌、半腱肌、半膜肌的肌腱及小腿三頭肌的肌腱，增強肌腱的伸展機能；並訓練膝關節內外側的靭帶，增強靭帶的堅靭性。爲將來的高踢腿動作作好準備，爲蹬腿或踢腿時膝關節內外兩側靭帶，所必須擔負的力量打好基礎。

圖　1
Fig. 1

110

APPENDIX: BASIC LEG TRAINING

I. LEG PRESSING

A. FRONT PRESSING — LEG DOWN-PUSHING

Movements:
1. Facing the tool for training (a table, chair, wall, windowsill or stall bar; the tools hereinafter are all referred to these), stand with both feet two small paces apart.
2. put the right heel on the tool at the level of the lower abdomen with the tip of the foot raised and the knee stretched; support the body with the left foot with its tip pointing to the tool for training and the knee straightened.
3. crossing the five fingers of each hand with those of other, push them down on the right knee; the eyes are looking at the tip of the right foot.
4. bend both elbows, lean the upper body forward, return to original position and then lean forward again (Fig. 1). After leaning and pressing the right leg several times, put it down and place the left one on the tool instead.

Purposes: To train the tendons of the femoral biceps, semi-tendinous, semimembranous and sural triceps muscles so as to enhance their stretching function; to train the ligaments on the inner and outer sides of the knee joints to enhance their tenacity; to get ready for the future high-snapping movemnts of the foots; to lay the foundation for the power to be undertaken by the ligaments on the inner and outer sides of the knee joints in straight-kicking or kicking.

Explanations:
1. When leaning the upper body forward and pressing the legs, the movements of leaning and rising should not be too quick, but stop for a while when leaning down before

111

說明：1. 上身前俯壓腿時，一起一俯的動作不要做得太快，應該在俯下時略停一會後再直起身來。

2. 俯壓的次數，可以根據自己的可能來決定。一般說，在初練階段壓十次到二十次，然後逐漸增加，最後是以時間計算而不以次數計算。

3. 俯壓的程度，初練階段不要壓得過低，過低了，會拉斷肌肉纖維的。鍛煉了一個時期，自己感到可以俯低時才壓低。

4. 正壓腿，經過一個時期的訓練，擱腳的高度也可漸漸加高，但不應超過胸部高度，否則，就不能成為壓腿了。

5. 正壓必須挺胸、直背、挺膝、坐胯（右腿胯部向右下坐）、身前探、腳勾緊。

乙　側壓──壓腿

動作：1. 離開訓練工具兩小步站立，身體右側對工具。

2. 右腳跟擱在工具上，高度同前，腳尖上翹，膝部挺直；左腳踏在地上，以腳掌內側對訓練工具，膝部挺直。

3. 左手叉腰，右手握拳，小臂（靠近腕部處）放在胯部外側。

4. 上身向右側彎屈，以右小臂壓腿，略停片刻後，復原，再彎屈（圖二）。然後換左腿側壓。腿部的訓練總是左右均行的，下面僅是一側的說明，不再提換腿了。

目的：除了繼續訓練正壓動作中的各組肌腱及靭帶外，對髂股靭帶、腹股溝靭帶、股闊筋膜及梨狀肌、長收肌的伸長

straightening the body.

2. the frequency of leaning and pressing can depend on your own ability: in general, you can press the legs 10 to 20 times at the beginning of training and then gradually increase the frequency; finally count the length of time and not the frequency.

3. as to the degree of leaning and pressing, don't press to low at the beginning, otherwise it will break the muscular fibres; after you have trained for a period and when you think you are able to lean lower, then press the leg lower.

4. if you have trained in the front pressing for a period, you can increase the height of the tool for putting your foot step by step, but it should not be higher than the chest, otherwise it cannot be referred to as leg pressing.

5. in front pressing, you should throw your chest out, straighten your back, stretch your knees, lower your thighs (lower the right thigh to the right), lean your body forward and pull your feet tight.

B. SIDE PRESSING — LEG PRESSING

Movements:

1. Stand away from the tool for training with both feet two small paces apart, the right side of the body facing the tool.

2. put the right heel on the tool at the same height as aforesaid with the tip of the foot raised and the knee stretched; stamp the left foot on the ground with the inner side of its sole facing the training tool and the knee stretched.

圖 2

Fig. 2

和外展性都能進行很有效的訓練，爲將來的外擺腿、側踢、側蹬等動作創造肌肉和韌帶伸縮如意的條件。同時由於上身的側屈，還鍛煉了腹外斜肌和腰肌以及腰背部的筋膜。

說明： 1. 側壓的要求是：挺胸、直背、挺膝、開胯（髖關節外展）、身側屈、脚勾緊。

2. 側壓經過一個時期的鍛煉之後，支撐腿的脚尖應逐漸外展，加大開胯的幅度。

3. 側壓到了後期，在增加高度時，左臂變爲屈肘上擧，右臂則垂於襠前，使上身側屈的幅度加大，用左手去碰或握右脚尖。這對上述的肌腱、韌帶、筋膜的訓練是相應地提高了一步（圖三）。

圖　3
Fig. 3

114

3. place the left foot at the waist, clench the right fist and put the right forearm (near the wrist) by the lateral side of the thigh.

4. bend the upper body to the right and press the leg with the right forearm; stop for a while, return the body to original position and bend it again (Fig. 2). Then side-press the left leg instead. The training in legs should always be evenly carried out on both legs. In the following, I shall only explain the training in one leg and no longer mention the changing of legs.

Purposes: In addition to continuing to train in tendons and ligaments mentioned in the front pressing, it can have very good effect on the training of the stretching and extension of the iliofemoral and inguinal ligaments, the femoral wide fasciae as well as the piriform and long adductor muscles so as to create the ideal conditions for the free extension and contraction of muscles and ligaments in the future movements of the legs, such as outward swinging, side kicks, side straight-kicking, etc.. At the same time, due to the side bending of the upper body, the abdominal external oblique and lumbar muscles and the fasciae on the lower back.

Explanations:

1. The requirements for side pressing are: throw the chest out, straighten the back, stretch the knees, open the hip (extend the hip joints outward), bend the body to one side and pull the feet tight.

2. after training in side pressing for a period, the tip of the supporting foot must gradually be extended outward so as to increase the scope of hip opening.

3. in the late period of side pressing when the height is increased, hold the left arm up with the elbow bent and hang the right arm in front of the crotch to increase the scope of the side bending of the upper body and to touch or hold the tip of the right foot with the left hand. Accoding this enhances the training of the abovementioned tendons, ligaments and fasciae (Fig. 3).

115

丙　斜壓——沉腿

動作： 1. 上身的右後方對訓練工具站立。

2. 右腳腳尖繃直，用腳掌內側擱在訓練工具上，使腿部內側朝下，膝部挺直；左腿膝部挺直，腳跟對訓練工具站立。

3. 兩手叉腰，虎口朝下，所謂反叉腰。

4. 上身向後仰，以沉壓右腿（圖四）。

目的： 訓練恥骨肌、長收肌、股薄肌、大收肌、股內肌、縫匠肌和股直肌的伸長以及小腿橫韌帶和十字韌帶的堅韌，為武術動作中的前後劈叉部份地作好準備；同時也加深地訓練了髖關節囊、髂股韌帶、股圓韌帶的彈性和滑潤性，促使髖關節的靈活，並對腹直肌也作了鍛煉。

說明： 1. 擱在訓練工具上的腿，腳尖務必繃直，使腳面伸平。

2. 上身向後的時候，
小腹必須向前挺凸，
否則，只仰胸彎腰不
會起沉壓動作的作用。

3. 斜壓訓練的高度，
開始時比正側壓要低
些，以後慢慢加高。

4. 沉壓次數與正壓同
，可多可少。

圖　4
Fig. 4

116

C. SLANTING PRESSING – LEG SINKING

Movements:

1. Stand with the right side of the back facing the training tool.
2. stretching the tip of the right foot, put the inner side of the sole on the training tool with the internal side of the leg facing down and the knee stretched; stretching the left knee, stand with the heel facing the tool.
3. place both hands at the waist with the tiger's mouths (the hollow between a thumb and a forefinger) facing down, which is known as arms placed reverse akimbo.
4. lean the upper body backward so as to sink and press the right leg (Fig. 4).

Purposes: To train in the extension of the pectineal, long adductor, gracile, major adductor, femoral internal, tailor's and femoral rectus muscles and in the tenacity of the crural transverse and crucial ligaments so as to get ready for the forward and backward splits in the movements of Chinese martial arts; at the same time to enhance the elascity and lubricity of the hip joint sacs, the iliofemoral and femoral round ligaments so as to make the hip joints agile and to train the abdominal rectus muscle.

Explanations:

1. The tip of the foot on the training tool must be stretch to make its face falt.
2. when leaning the upper body back, throw the lower abdomen out, otherwise only by throwing the chest out and bending the waist, you cannot obtain the effect of sinking and pressing.
3. at the beginning, the height for slanting pressing must be lower than side or front pressing and is to be increased gradually.
4. as in front pressing, the frequency of sinking can be varied.

丁 反壓——反抬腿

動作： 1.面對訓練工具站立；兩手扶工具，上身略前俯。

2.左腿支持身體，膝部挺直，脚尖對工具；右腿由助手握住由身後向上抬起，膝挺直，繃脚尖。

3.高抬之後，徐徐放下，放到與助手的肩齊平時，再徐徐上抬，如此反復進行（圖五）。

目的： 訓練髖關節向後反轉的靈活性，加強大小腿前面的股直肌，股四頭肌，縫匠肌，髂腰肌以及腹股溝韌帶的伸展，並使闊筋膜的擴張性加大。

說明： 1.當助手抬腿的時候，練習者的上身要向後仰，借以訓練腰脊的柔軟性。

2.如果沒有助手。自己持一種較高的家具和兩種較矮的家具，兩手扶助較矮的，把腿反攔在較高的上面，伸肘挺身向後屈腰，也能進行訓練。

壓腿訓練，除了上面的按、壓、沉、抬的正、側、斜、反

圖 5

Fig. 5

118

D. REVERSE PRESSING — LEG REVERSE LIFTING

Movements:
1. Stand facing the training tool; hold the tool with both hands, leaning the upper body slightly forward.
2. support the body with the left leg with the knee stretched and the tip of the foot pointing to the tool; with the assistance of the aide, lift the right leg up behind the body with the knee stretched and the tip of the foot also stretched.
3. after the foot is lifted high, drop it slowly down to the level of the aide's shoulders, and then slowly lift it up again, repeating the movement in this way (Fig. 5).

Purposes: To train tin the agility of the hip joints to turn backward, to enhance the extension of the femoral rectus muscles, femoral quadriceps muscles and tailors muscles at the fronts of the legs, the iliolumbar muscles and the inguinal ligaments and to increase the expansion of the wise fasciae.

Explanations:
1. When the aide is lifting your leg up, lean the upper body back so as to train the flexibility of the lumbar spine.
2. If there is no aide, get one higher piece of furniture and two lower pieces of furniture; holding the lower ones with both hands and putting the leg on the higher one, you can train by stretching the elbow, throwing your body out and bending your waist backward.

When training in the leg pressing, in addition to the basic techniques of front down-pushing, side pressing, slanting sinking and reverse lifting as aforesaid, there are other movements in combination with them, such as leaning the body forward and holding the leg (which is supporting the body) in side pressing , leaning the body back in front pressing, etc.. The purpose is to train the tendons of another part at the same time when training the tendons of one part. But this is not the main purpose of training, so I shall not illustrate them.

等最基本的方法之外，還有結合這四種方法而進行的動作。如側壓加上俯身抱腿（支持身體的那條腿）、正壓加上仰體等等動作。其目的是在訓練某一部分肌腱的同時，附帶訓練一下另一部分的肌腱，但這不是主要的訓練目的，所以不舉例說明了。

二、搬　腿

甲　吻靴

動作： 1.右腿屈膝略蹲，左腿前伸，腿尖翹起，脚跟着地。

2.上身前俯，右手握住左脚內側，左手握住左脚外側(圖六)。

3.雙手用勁向後拉，上身盡量前俯，用嘴吻脚尖(圖七)。

4.上身仰起，雙臂伸直，接着再做第二次。

目的： 主要是訓練小腿後部的腓腸肌，比目魚肌及跟腱的伸長性；同時也訓練了小腿前部的脛骨前肌腱的收縮性。另外，由於屈伸下蹲，也訓練了腿部肌肉的力量與彈性。

說明： 1.搬腿吻靴必須挺胸、直背、塌腰、身前探、挺膝、坐胯、收肘、咬脚尖。

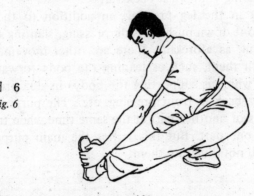

圖　6
Fig. 6

120

II. FOOT PULLING

A. SHOE KISSING

Movements:
1. Bending the right knee to squat slightly down, stretch the left leg forward with the tip of the foot raised and the heel touching the ground.
2. lean the upper body forward to hold the inner side of the left foot with the right hand and the outer side of the left foot with the left hand (Fig. 6).
3. pull the foot back forcefully with both hands, leaning the upper body forward as far as you can to kiss the tip of the foot with the mouth (Fig. 7).
4. raise the upper body and stretch both arms. Then go on with the second time.

Purposes: Mainly for training in the extension of the gastrocnemius and soleus muscles at the back of a shank and the heel tendons; at the same time, to train in the contraction of the muscle tendons in front of a tibia at the front of a shank. In addition, due to the squatting by bending the knee, the strength and elasticity of the muscles of the legs are also trained.

Explanations:
1. In shoe kissing, throw the chest out, straighten the back, lower the waist, lean the body forward, stretch the knees, lower the hip, draw the elbows in and bit the tip of the foot.

圖 7
Fig. 7

121

2. 搬腿吻靴也可在工具上進行，支撐腿伸直，不必屈蹲。

3. 吻靴訓練比較艱苦，開始的時候，可以先以頭頂去「頂」
   腳尖，然後再進一步用前額去「叩」腳尖，繼而以嘴
   「吻」，最後以下顎去「拂」腳尖。所謂「頂、叩、
   吻、拂腿練到，筋長一分力量巧」（華拳譜）。

乙　臥靴（左、右臥）

右臥靴：

動作：1. 左腳伸前一步，腳尖翹起，腳跟着地，右腿屈膝略蹲。

2. 上身前俯，左手反叉後腰際，右手滿握左腳，手心與
   腳心相合，上身趁勢左轉（圖八）。

3. 上身倒下，以身體的右側臥在左腿上，頭頂碰着腳尖
   （圖九）。

4. 回至第二動作，再繼續下臥。這是所謂「右臥靴」。

圖　8
Fig. 8

2. shoe kissing can also be done on a tool; in this case, stretch the supporting leg without the necessity to squat down.
3. shoe kissing is rather arduous. At the beginning, first push the tip of the foot with your vertex, next knock at the tip with your forehead and then kiss it with your mouth; finally stroke it with your chin. There goes the saying that "if you can attain the results of leg training of pushing, knocking, kissing and stroking, your tendons will be a little lengthened and you can use your strength cleverly" (Hua Chuan Guide).

B. SHOE LYING-ON (LEFT AND RIGHT LYING)

SHOE LYING-ON (RIGHT MODE)

Movements:
1. Stretch the left foot a step forward with its tip raised and its heel touching the ground and bend the right knee to squat a little down.
2. lean the upper body forward, placing the reversely at the back of the left loin and holding the left foot with the right hand with its palm close to the sole; turn the upper body left accordingly (Fig. 8).
3. drop the upper body with its right side lying on the left leg and the vertex touching the tip of the left foot (Fig. 9).
4. return to the second movement and continue to lie down. This is known as "Right Shoe Lying-on".

 9

Fig. 9

左臥靴：

1. 同上述動作。

2. 上身向右轉，以身體的左側對左脚，左手抱於右脅處，右臂屈肘上擧（圖十）。

3. 上身倒下，以身體的左側臥在左腿上，右手滿握左脚，頭頂靠近脚尖（圖十一）。

4. 右手放鬆，回至第二動作後再作第二次。這是所謂「左臥靴」。

目的： 一方面訓練腿部的肌腱和靭帶，一方面訓練腹外斜肌、背闊肌，岡下肌等肌肉羣，間接地也鍛煉了腰部的柔軟性。所以華拳譜裏說：「左右把靴臥，練腿又使腰」。

說明： 1. 臥靴時，必須以身體的側面倒臥腿上，不可用胸部俯在腿上。

2. 先用身體右側臥，做了數次之後，再向另一側進行，不要做一次右側臥，
接着就做左側臥。

圖 10
Fig. 10

SHOE LYING-ON (LEFT MODE)

Movements:
1. The same as aforesaid.
2. turn the upper body right with its left side facing the left foot, the left hand holding the right armpit and the right arm held up with the elbow bent (Fig. 10).
3. drop the upper body with its left side lying on the left leg, the right hand holding the left foot and the vertex close to the tip of the foot (Fig. 11).
4. loosen the right hand and return to the second movement to repeat once more. This is socalled "Left Shoe Lying-on".

Purposes: On one hand, to train the muscle tendons and ligaments of the legs; on the other hand, to train such muscle groups as the abdominal external oblique, dorsal wide and infraspinal muscles, thus indirectly training in the flexibility of the waist. Therefore, the Hua Chuan Guide reads: "Lying left and right on the shoe, your legs and waist are trained."

Explanations:
1. In shoe lying-on, drop the side of the body onto the leg and don't lean the chest onto the leg.
2. First do the exercise with the right side lying on the leg several times before doing with the other side; don't do it once alternately with the two sides.

圖 11
Fig. 11

丙　抱靴

動作：1. 左腿屈膝向前提起。

2. 左手抱住左膝脛骨，右手滿握左腳。

3. 像抱東西那樣，把左腳盡量朝上抱起，使左膝內側緊貼在左乳上部（圖十二）。

目的：擴大髖關節的運動面。

說明：1. 訓練抱靴時，必須挺胸、直背、支撐腿挺直、站穩。

2. 站立的時間可以從二分鐘增到五分鐘，借以增强單腿獨立的平衡能力。

圖　12
Fig. 12

C. SHOW HOLDING

Movements:
1. Bend the left leg and lift it up.
2. hold the left tibia with the left hand and grab the left foot with the right hand.
3. hold the left foot up as high as you can as if holding something in the arms, putting the internal side of the left knee close to the upper part of the left breast (Fig. 12).

Purposes: To enlarge the scope of the movement of the hip joints.

Explanations:
1. In shoe holding, throw the chest out, straighten the back, stretch the supporting leg and stand firm.
2. the time for standing can be increased from 2 minutes to 5 minutes so as to enhance the balancing ability to stand singly on one leg.

丁　端靴

動作： 1. 同抱靴，左手反叉左腰。

2. 左腿向前上方伸出，膝部挺直，右手滿握左脚，左脚
　外側對前方（圖十三）。

3. 回復抱靴狀，接着再做第二次。

目的： 與正面高腿相同，但也有訓練平衡感覺的目的。

說明： 1. 訓練端靴時必須挺胸、直背、收胯、支撐腿挺直、站
　穩；

2. 「端靴」的「端」就是端詳的意思，因之脚的高度至
　少應與眼平，目光平視脚尖。

圖　13
Fig. 13

128

D. SHOE UPHOLDING

Movements:

1. The same as in shoe holding, placing the left hand reverse at the left loin.
2. stretch the left leg up to the front with the knee stretched and grab the left foot with the right hand with the outer side of the foot facing forward (Fig. 13).
3. return to shoe holding, then go on with a second time.

Purposes: The same as in the front leg lifting, but also to train the sense of balance.

Explanations:

1. Training in shoe upholding, throw the chest out, straighten the back, draw the hip back, stretch the supporting leg and stand firm.
2. Shoe upholding has also the meaning of looking at the shoe carefully, therefore the foot must be held up at least to the level of the eyes so as to look levelly at the tip of the foot.

三、懸 腿

甲　前懸

動作： 1. 右手扶右側的訓練工具，左手叉腰。

2. 左腿屈膝提起，腳尖綳直（圖十四）。

3. 腳尖綳直着向前緩緩伸出（圖十五）。

4. 左腿屈膝回至第二動作後再繼續前伸。

目的： 訓練腿部肌肉的伸展能力和控制能力，爲某些拳術中的脫手朝天蹬等靜止性蹬腿正型動作奠定基礎。

說明： 前懸分綳腳與蹬腳（翹腳尖）兩種。蹬腳的練習方法是在腿伸出時腳尖要上翹並用腳跟蹬出。這兩種方法必須輪換練習，不可偏廢。正像華拳譜裏說：「踢足（就是綳直腳面）長前筋，蹬腿拉後腱」，這說明兩者的訓練效能是相應結合的。

圖　14
Fig. 14

III. LEG HANGING

A. FRONT HANGING

Movements:

1. Hold the training tool on the right with the right hand, placing the left hand at the waist.
2. bend the left knee and lift the foot up with its tip stretched (Fig. 14).
3. stretch the foot out slowly forward with its tip stretched (Fig. 15).
4. bend the left knee to return to the second movement and then continue to stretch it forward.

Purposes: To train in the extending ability and controlling ability of the muscles of thelegs so as to lay the foundation for the regular movements of static kicks, such as Kicking toward the Sky by Letting the Foot Slip Out of the Hand in certain Chinese boxing schools.

Explanations: There are two types of Front Hanging: one with the foot stretched and the other with the tip of the foot raised. The training . method in the latter is to raise the tip of the foot and kick out with the heel when stretching the leg out. You must alternately train in the two types and you cannot emphasize one at the expense of the other. Just as what the HuaChuan Guide says, "kicking with the face of the foot stretched can lengthen the front sinews, while kicking with the tip of the foot raised

圖 15
Fig. 15

131

乙　側懸

動作：1.右手扶持訓練工具，左手叉腰或垂於襠前。

　　　2.左腿屈膝、繃脚向左側提起（圖十六）。

　　　3.左腿向左側緩緩伸出（圖十七）。

　　　4.回至第二動作後再繼續進行第二次。

目的：同前。

說明：1.側懸腿時，必須使腿正向側方，不能有絲毫偏斜。

　　　2.上身端正挺胸，不能側轉傾斜。

　　　3.側懸腿同樣可分繃脚和蹬脚兩種，可輪換練習。

圖　16
Fig. 16

132

can pull the rear tendons", which shows the training efficacy of these two types is relevantly combined.

B. SIDE HANGING

Movements:
1. Hold the training tool with the right hand, placing the left hand at the waist or hang it down in front of the crotch.
2. bend the left knee and lift the foot up to the left with the foot stretched (Fig. 16).
3. stretch the left leg slowly out to the left (Fig. 17).
4. return to the second movement and go on with a second time.

Purposes: The same as aforesaid.

Explanations:
1. In side hanging, you must face the lifted leg right to one side without any slanting.
2. keep the upper body upright and throw the chest out; you cannot turn or incline it to one side.
3. side hanging also has two types: one with the foot stretched and the other with the foot raised. You cantrain alternately in them.

圖 17
Fig. 17

133

丙　斜懸

動作： 1. 與 2. 與側懸腿相同。

3. 向左側斜後方緩緩伸出，脚尖繃直，脚部的內側朝下，外側朝上（圖十八）。

4. 回至第二動作後再做第二次。

目的： 訓練腿部肌肉的外展，伸張和控制能力。

說明： 1. 訓練斜懸腿時，上身很容易前俯，這是要特別注意的

2. 斜懸腿的高度，一般來說，是不太容易加高的，練習時不要過於心急，要循序漸進。

3. 斜懸腿的訓練只有繃脚一種，如果改為蹬脚，那就等於是擴大側懸角度的蹬脚式側懸。

圖　18
Fig. 18

C. SLANTING HANGING

Movements:
   1 & 2. The same as in Side Hanging.
   2. stretch the left leg slantingly out slowly to the left back-side with the tip of the foot stretched, its inner side downward and its outer side upward (Fig. 18).
   4. return to the second movement and go on with a second time.
Purposes: To train in the extending ability, stretching ability and controlling ability of the muscles of the legs.
Explanations:
   1. When training in slanting hanging, the upper body is liable to lean forward, which you should particularly guard against.
   2. in general, the height in slanting hanging is not easy to raise, so you should not be too impatient in training but should progress step by step.
   3. the training in slanting hanging has only one type; the one with the foot stretched; if the foot is raised instead, the posture can be called the Straight-kicking-type Side Hanging which enlarges the angle of side hanging.

丁　高懸

高懸腿訓練是在正、側懸腿有了進展的情況下才進行的；換句話說，即是正、側懸腿的極點。它的動作和正、側懸腿完全相同，其高度却有兩樣：正面高懸應該像壓腿訓練中的正面收胯式高腿那樣，能使脚尖碰着前額；側面高懸應該像側面收胯式高腿那樣，能使脚尖碰着耳際上部。當然，如果按這樣的要求來練習高懸腿是極不容易的，但不能不向這個要求努力，至少做到離這要求不遠。高懸腿一般只限於正側面，同時也只限於蹬脚式。斜懸腿雖也可以高懸，但受股骨大小粗隆和髖骨接連的限制，難以達到極點。高懸腿是增强腿部肌肉和髖關節收縮、伸展、柔韌、靈活、外張等性能的訓練，也是肌肉控制性能的進一步的訓練。

四、踢　腿
甲　前踢

動作： 1. 雙手叉腰，右脚上前一步，左脚在後。

2. 左脚向前上方額前踢起，脚尖幾乎碰到額骨(圖十九)。

3. 左脚落下與右脚並攏後即向前一步，使右脚在後。

4. 右脚向額前踢起。如此輪換下去。

說明： 1. 踢起時，腰部不要彎曲，要挺胸，上身前傾的幅度不要過大。

圖　19
Fig. 19

D. HIGH HANGING

The training in high hanging can only be carried out after you have made progress in front or side hanging; in other words, high hanging is the extremity of front or side hanging. Its movements are exactly the same as in front or side hanging, but the heights are different: in front high hanging, you should enable the tip of the foot to touch the forehead, just as in lifting the foot high with the hip drawn back; in side high hanging, you should enable the tip to touch the upper part of the edge of the ear, just as in lifting the foot high sidewise with the hip drawn back. Of course, if you are to train in high hanging in accordance with these requirements, it is very uneasy, but you have no alternative but to strive for the purpose. At least, you should get near to the standard. In general, high hanging is only confined to front or side hanging and only with the foot raised. Although the leg can be lifted high in slanting hanging, you cannot reach the extremity due to the limitation of the connections between the major and minor protuberances of the femoral bones and hipbone. High hanging is the training in such functions as contraction, extension, flexibility and tenacity, agility and outstretching of the muscles of the legs and hip joints. It is also the further training in the controlling ability of muscles.

IV. FOOT SNAPPING

A. FORWARD SNAPPING

Movements:
1. Standing akimbo, move the right foot a step forward, keeping the left one behind.
2. snap the left foot up forward to the forehead with its tip almost touching the frontal bone (Fig. 19).
3. drop the left foot, bring it close to the right one and then move the left foot a step forward, keeping the right one behind.

2.上身不要後仰，以免跌倒。

3.踏地的一腳的膝部要挺直，腳尖正對前方，腳跟不能
　因踢起動作而離地。

4.踢起的腿的膝部也要挺直，腳尖翹起。

5.踢時也可以繃直腳尖。

6.踢時也可以不叉腰，而將兩手握拳側平舉。這樣，比
　叉腰的前踢要容易些，因為容易維持身體的平衡。

7.前踢腿應該以小腿用力上擺而去帶動大腿，這樣才能
　使踢腿的速度和力量得到鍛煉。

乙　斜掛

動作：1.同前踢。

　　　2.左腳向右耳旁踢去（圖二十）。

　　　3.與 4. 同前踢。

說明：1.踢起時，面部宜
　　　向左（如果踢左腳
　　　，面部就向左偏）
　　　或向右略偏。

　　　2.踢時以兩手握拳
　　　側平舉的姿勢為最
　　　妥。

圖　20
Fig. 20

138

4. snap the right foot up forward to the forehead. Go on alternately with the exercise.

Explanations:

1. When snapping the foot, don't bend the waist, but throw the chest out and con't overlean the upper body forward.
2. don't lean the body backward lest you should fall.
3. the knee of the foot on the ground must be stretched with the tip of the foot pointing to the very front, don't lift the heel away from the ground when snapping another foot up.
4. the knee of the snapped leg must also be stretched with the tip of the foot raised.
5. When snapping, the tip of the foot can also be stretched.
6. When snapping, it is allowed. not to place the hands at the waist, but hold them levelly at the height of the shoulders with the fists clenched. Then, it is easier to snap the foot forward than placing the hands at the waist because it is easy to keep the balance of the body.
7. In foot forward snapping, you must exert the force of the shank and swing it up, bringing the thigh with it. Only by doing so can you have trained yourself in the speed and strength of foot snapping.

B. SLANTING SNAPPING

Movements:

1. The same as in Forward Snapping.
2. snap the left foot to beside the right ear (Fig. 20).
3 & 4. the same as in forward snapping.

Explanations:

1. When snapping the foot up, incline the face to the left to right (if the left foot is snapped up, incline the face to the left).
2. When snapping, it is the best to hold both hands levelly at the height of the shoulders with the fists clenched.

丙 側踢

動作：1. 兩手握拳，但不要緊握，右腳上前一步，腳尖略向右
外側偏斜，上身右轉，身體左側向前，左拳垂於身前，
右拳上舉，肘微屈，左腳在後。

2. 左腳向左耳上方踢去，腳尖微碰頭部（圖二十一）。

3. 左腳向前落下，腳尖略向左外側偏斜，上身變為左轉，
身體右側向前，右拳垂在身前，左拳由左側下方向後
繞於頭上，環屈肘。

4. 開始踢右腳。

說明：側踢只有翹腳尖的一種踢法。踢時兩腿必須挺直，並必
須收胯，才能達到
目的。在開始練習
時，可以踢得高一
些，就是使腳尖向
頭頂踢去。

圖 21
Fig. 21

C. SIDEWISE SNAPPING

Movements:

1. Clenching both fists but don't clench them tightly, move the right foot a step forward with its tip pointing slantingly to the right external side; turning the upper body right to face its left part forward and hanging the left fist in front of the body, hold the right fist up with the elbow slightly bent, keeping the left foot behind.
2. snap the left foot toward the upper part of the left ear, its tip slightly touching the head (Fig. 21).
3. drop the left foot forward with its tip pointingly slightly slantingly to the left external side; turning the upper body left to face its right part forward and hanging the right fist in front of the body, revolve the left fist backward from the left lower side and place it above the head with the elbow bent.
4. begin to snap the right foot up.

Explanations: Sidewise snapping has only one type: the one with the tip of the foot raised. When snapping, both legs must be stretched and the hip must be drawn back. Only by doing so can you attain your purpose. At the beginning of the exercise, you can snap the foot higher, that is to say, snap the tip of the foot against the vertex.

丁　外擺

動作：1.兩手握拳側平舉，左脚上一步，右脚在後。

2.右腿由後向身體左側踢起。

3.右腿經面部向身體右側擺過（圖二十二）。

4.右脚在左脚邊踏地。

5.右脚上一步，擺左腿，如此輪換。

說明：1.外擺時很容易使小腹內縮和上身前傾，這樣就不能使髖關節充分靈活，因此，腰腹必須挺直。

2.如果擺右腿的話，當腿擺至身體右側時，必須與體側成一百八十度的直面，不要在擺至右前方時就落地，因爲這樣就不能擴大肌肉的振幅。

圖 22
Fig. 22

142

D. OUTWARD SWINGING

Movements:
1. Holding both hands levelly at the height of the shoulders with the fist clenched, move the left foot a step forward, keeping the right foot behind.
2. snap the right leg up to the left of the body from behind.
3. swing the right leg by front of the face to the right of the body (Fig. 22).
4. stamp the right foot on the ground beside the left one.
5. move the right foot a step forward and swing the left leg. Do the exercise alternately in this way.

Explanations:
1. In outward swinging, you are liable to shrink the lower abdomen in and lean the upper body forward. Thus the hip joints cannot be fully made free. Therefore, you must stretch your waist and abdomen.
2. If the right leg is swung, when the leg is swung to the right of the body, it must be at the same plane with the right side of the body. Don't drop it on the ground when it only gets to the right front side bcause this cannot enlarge the amplitude of muscles.

戊 裏合

動作：1.同外擺動作。

2.右腿向前踢起，但不要像前踢那樣高（圖二十三）。

3.右腿向身後蕩回，上身隨之右轉。

4.右腿從右側上踢經面部向左側迴環落地與左脚並攏（圖二十四），上身隨之左轉正對前方。

5.換左腿做。

說明：1.裏合腿前踢時不要像前踢那樣用力。

2.當右腿從前方蕩下擺回來的時候，上身雖隨之右轉，但左脚尖仍正對前方，不能有所移動。

3.在腿蕩回進行裏合的時候，最容易使上身前屈和膝部彎屈，這要特別注意。

圖 23
Fig. 23

E. INWARD BRINGING

Movements:

1. The same as in outward swinging.
2. snap the ring leg up forward, but don't snap it up as high as in forward snapping (Fig. 23).
3. swing the right leg back to the backside of the body and turn the upper body right accordingly.
4. snap the right foot up from the right, revolve it by front of the face, drop it to the ground and bring it close to the left one (Fig. 24), turning the upper body left accordingly to the very front.
5. do the exercise with the left leg instead.

Explanations:

1. When snapping the foot forward in inward bringing, don't snap it so forcefully as in forward snapping.
2. when swinging the right leg back from front, turn the upper body right accordingly, but still point the tip of the left foot to the very front and cannot move it.
3. When bringing the leg back close to the other one, you are most liable to lean the upper body forward and bend the knee, which you should particularly guard against.

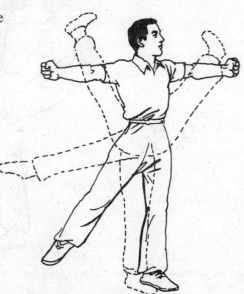

圖 24
Fig. 24

145

己 倒打

動作： 1. 兩手握拳側平舉，上左脚，踢起右腿，脚尖使之碰到前額，如同前踢腿動作。

2. 右腿蕩下向後上方踢起，用脚掌去打頭部，此時，上身屈腰後仰以迎右腿（圖二十五）。

3. 右腿落下時上前一步，換左脚做。

說明： 1. 倒打動作在華拳譜裏叫做「倒打紫金冠」，這說明對這個訓練的要求一定要打到頭部。

2. 倒打的時候膝部可以彎屈，但支持身體的一腿不能彎屈。

圖 25
Fig. 25

146

F. REVERSE SNAPPING

Movements:
1. Holding both fists at the level of the shoulders, move the left foot forward and snap the right foot up to enable its tip to touch the forehead as in forward snapping.
2. swing the right leg down and snap it up to the upper backside to strike the sole at the head; at this time, bend the upper body backward to meet the right foot (Fig. 25).
3. drop the right foot, move it a step forward and do the exercise with the left foot instead.

Explanations:
1. In the Hua Chuan Guide, reverse snapping is called "reverse snapping at the purple golden crown", which proves that this training requires to hit the head.
2. In reverse snapping, the knee can be bent, but the supporting leg cannot be bent.
3. When snapping the foot forward in reverse snapping, it is not necessary to reach the forehead.
4. at the beginning of the training in reverse snapping, you can do the exercise by holding a wall, table, chair or stool, etc. with both hands.

The movements of forward snapping, slanting snapping, sidewise snapping, outward swinging, inward bringing and reverse snapping in the training of leg snapping are all the moving training of the muscles, ligaments and joints after such static training as leg pressing or foot pulling. Their purposes are to enable the muscle tendons and ligaments to take direct part in the movements so as to train in their kinetic functions, in their elascity, flexibility, extension, amplitude and power. Therefore, the Hua Chuan Guide reads: "It is no use to press but not to slip, while you will be as awkward as an ox if you simply press legs but not slip them". As to the frequency of the snapping in these six techniques, it will be rather harsh for the beginners to snap one hundred times in each exercise

3.倒打的前踢也不一定要踢到前額。

4.倒打在初步訓練階段，兩手可以扶着牆、桌、凳或椅
 等物件來進行。

踢腿訓練的前踢、斜掛、側踢、外擺、裏合、倒打等動作
都是腿部肌肉、靭帶和關節經過壓腿、搬腿等靜止性訓練之後
的活動性訓練。這種活動性訓練的目的，是使那些肌腱和靭帶
直接地投入運動，訓練它們的運動性能，鍛煉它們的彈性、鬆
弛、伸展、振幅和力量。所以華拳譜裏說：「壓而不溜不中用，
溜而不壓笨如牛。」這六種踢腿方法的次數，如果按「腿溜百
遍汗滿流」的要求，對初步練習的人來說，是有點苛刻的。初
練者一般可以踢四十次，兩腿各踢二十次，以後再逐漸地增加
到一百次。

until one sweats a great deal. The beginners are generally allowed to snap forty times, twenty times for each leg, and gradually increase the frequency to one hundred times.